SEXUALITY

GOD'S GIFT

FOR ADOLESCENTS

ANN CANNON

Family Touch.

Nashville, Tennessee

7808-43
ISBN: 0-8054-9968-7

Dewey Decimal Classification: 155.3
Subject Heading: SEX EDUCATION//SEXUAL BEHAVIOR
Printed in the United States of America

Scripture quotations are from the *New American Standard Bible*.
© The Lockman Foundation, 1960, 1962, 1963, 1968, 1971, 1972,
1973, 1975, 1977. Used by permission.

Family Touch Press
127 Ninth Avenue, North
Nashville, TN 37234

Contents

CHAPTER 1

Body Talk

I will give thanks to Thee, for I am fearfully and wonderfully made.

Psalm 139:14

Ches raced across the finish line. Suddenly the prettiest girl in school leaped from the spectator stands and dashed toward Ches. In front of everyone she planted a large, red kiss on his mouth. Ches awoke with a jolt!

He lay in the darkness taking inventory of his body and wondering, *What's happening to me? I'm always tired. I knock over everything. I walk into doors and people. It's like my body doesn't listen to me. I can't even think straight.*

Ches recalled how grumpy and ugly he felt yesterday. Last week he thought life was great.

Are you like Ches? Confused by new thoughts? Excited about your growing body? Frightened by constant aches and pains? Concerned about how you look? Cautious about telling others your fears?

Welcome to adolescence. You are not alone! Other young men and women have similar fears, thoughts, and feelings. Like you, they hesitate to talk about them. This book can help you understand what is happening to your body and your mind as each grows sexually.

What's Happening?

Test your knowledge of your physical changes. Write *true* or *false* by each statement. Look for the answers as you read this chapter.

_____ 1. Puberty is the time when you act less like a child and more like an adult.

_____ 2. Both sexes have male and female hormones in their bodies.

_____ 3. Circumcision is strictly a religious ritual performed on male babies.

_____ 4. Sperm cells are very delicate.

_____ 5. Females have a sex organ similar to the male penis.

_____ 6. A girl cannot become pregnant while she is menstruating.

_____ 7. The Bible condemns masturbation.

_____ 8. Hormones affect your moods, thoughts, and feelings about yourself, as well as your sexual development.

_____ 9. Within marriage, sexual intercourse is the most intimate form of communication.

_____ 10. Sexuality refers to your sexual gender.

Your New and Improved Body

Everything is changing. This period of change is called adolescence. You no longer think or act like a child. Now you want to think and act like an adult. During adolescence you get caught in between. Gradually you will leave childlike actions behind and accept more adult

5

values and actions. *(Number 1 is false. Read on.)*

Puberty occurs during adolescence. In puberty the sex organs begin to grow and function. Girls launch into puberty between the ages of eight and twelve. Boys get started later, usually around ten to fourteen. Don't worry if you don't fit into that age range. Each person's body operates on its own schedule. Your biological time clock will tell your body when to start growing.

Puberty is not a disease; it does not need a cure. It just needs to be understood. This book is designed to help you understand your sexual development. It is not like the sex education courses at school. In addition to the physical facts, you will find ideas based on the Bible for setting your own moral standards. Also look for biblical truths related to your questions and concerns.

You will notice that the correct words for the body parts and their functions are used instead of slang. Slang degrades sex and sex organs. Your sexual development is a positive, important event. You may feel uncomfortable at first using the correct words. That's normal, but try anyway.

Let's Get Physical!

Puberty starts as an inside job. Two major glands in the body trigger the release of growth-producing hormones. One of these glands is the pea-size *pituitary* located in the brain. It acts as a main control center for releasing hormones. The hypothalamus gland near the pituitary gland plays a secondary role.

These hormones affect the body in different ways. First, they get a body's sexual growth started. Then they keep the body's sexual functions running smoothly.

Estrogen and progesterone are the major hormones needed for girls. The main male hormone is testosterone. Traces of both male and female *hormones* are found in every person. *(Number 2 is true.)* Boys, however, have

more testosterone. Girls have more estrogen and progesterone.

Let's look at each sex's physical changes.

What Happens to Young Men?

The pituitary gland stimulates male sex glands called
testes. These glands produce both testosterone and
sperm. Growth of the male sex organs can occur as early
as age ten or as late as thirteen or fourteen. The first
noticeable sign of sexual change is growth of pubic hair
around the penis.

The *penis* is the main male sex organ. Its tip, called
the *glans,* is highly sensitive. At birth a foreskin, or thin
layer of skin, covers the glans. In the Old Testament this
foreskin was removed to identify a man who followed
God. The procedure is called circumcision. Today most
male babies are routinely circumcised at birth.
Circumcision is not considered medically necessary. Most
parents consent to circumcision because of religious, aes-
thetic, psychological, or cultural reasons. *(Number 3 is
false.)*

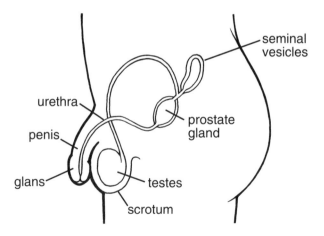

A small slit at the end of the penis is called the meatus. Both semen and urine leave the body through the *urethra* and this opening, but never at the same time.

The spongy tissue inside the penis contains numerous blood vessels. Usually the penis is soft and limp. When sexually aroused, however, the blood vessels swell with blood, and the penis stiffens. This is called an erection. There is no muscle or bone in the penis.

Below the penis near the body is the *scrotum*. This loose bag-like membrane holds the testes or testicles. The testicles produce sperm cells. Sperm can be damaged by extreme heat and cold. To protect these delicate cells the scrotum pulls the testicles into the warmth of the body when it is cold. When it's hot, the scrotum hangs lower, moving the sperm away from body heat. *(Number 4 is true.)*

Because God created humans with the ability to have sexual relations at any time within marriage, the penis becomes erect when aroused. The testicles produce sperm all the time.

A mature *sperm* is the male's cell needed to fertilize the female's egg. Together they produce a baby. Mature sperm leave the testicles through a small tube called the vas deferens. This tube carries the sperm to the urethra and out the body.

Inside the male body are two pouch-shaped organs called *seminal vesicles*. Above these is the *prostate* gland. Both produce *semen*. Semen combines with sperm in the urethra to help the sperm move easily. In a half teaspoon of semen are 250-500 million sperm cells.

About half a teaspoon of semen spurts out during ejaculation. This happens as a man reaches a climax or orgasm. Shortly after ejaculation the penis grows soft and returns to its normal size.

During puberty hormones set in motion other bodily changes in males. Hair usually grows on the chest and underarms. The soft fuzz of facial hair grows coarse and thick. Skin changes produce excess oil which may result in acne with some boys. Boys seem to have more trouble with acne than girls.

Hormones also cause the voice box to develop. For about a year a boy's voice gradually deepens. During this time boys are often embarrassed by voices that squeak unexpectedly.

Muscle development in arms and legs also occurs because of hormone activity. Shoulders get broader and hips grow more narrow.

What Happens to Young Women?

For boys, the *pituitary* gland starts the growth process. For girls, the pituitary gland stimulates the ovaries to produce estrogen. Estrogen sparks growth in female sex organs. Then on a regular cycle estrogen keeps these organs working.

Unlike boys, most of the sex organs of a female are inside her body. The *vulva* involves the only external female sex organs. The two outer lips of the vulva are called the *labia.* These fleshy folds protect the other parts. Two thin inside lips cover the openings to the urinary canal and the vagina.

Partially hidden under the covering of the labia at the front of the vulva is a small, knob-like organ called the *clitoris.* It is similar to the penis in shape and tissue development only smaller. During sexual arousal the clitoris swells with blood and grows extremely sensitive. Of the sex organs on both males and females, the clitoris is the only one that has no reproductive function. Its only job is to provide sexual pleasure for a woman. *(Number 5 is true.)*

Directly below the clitoris is the opening for the *urethra.* This tube goes to the bladder. It provides a way for urine to leave the body.

Below the urethra is a larger opening to the vagina. Sometimes a thin membrane, called the *hymen,* covers this entrance. Years ago an unbroken hymen meant the

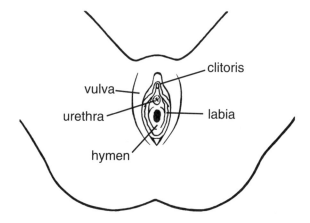

girl was a virgin. In this age of active athletics a torn hymen can occur. An untorn hymen is no longer a test of virginity.

Inside a girl's body are her other sexual organs. The *vagina* is a female's major sex organ. This muscular tube varies in length and is extremely flexible. Not only can the vagina stretch to hold a man's erect penis, but it also expands during the birth of a baby. At the top of the vagina is the *cervix*. This small canal connects the vagina to the uterus. It gathers the male's semen from the vagina so it will not flow back out.

The *uterus* is a hollow, pear-shaped muscle about the size of a fist. During puberty the uterus actually doubles in size. In pregnancy the uterus holds and feeds a new life in the womb during its nine months of formation.

On either side of the uterus are *fallopian tubes* and ovaries. Each almond-shaped *ovary* contains thousands of immature eggs. The *egg* is the female's reproductive cell needed to make a baby. The narrow fallopian tubes provide a passageway for the egg to get to the uterus.

During puberty, hormones stimulate the ovaries to

begin to release ripe eggs on a regular cycle. This release is called ovulation. After breaking out of the ovary the egg travels down the fallopian tube. During this journey a male sperm may penetrate the egg following sexual intercourse. If the egg becomes fertilized, it continues into the uterus where it grows into a baby.

During the egg's release, hormones also tell the uterus to prepare for a fertilized egg. A blood-filled lining coats the inside of the uterus. This lining is prepared to nourish a fertilized egg that will grow into a baby.

If the egg is not fertilized, however, the lining is not needed. The uterus lining breaks away and passes through the vagina and out of the body. This disposal of the lining is called menstruation or a girl's period.

Menstruation usually begins during the teen years. It continues until a woman is in her late forties or fifties. The menstrual cycle usually takes place every twenty-eight days. At the time the egg breaks out of the ovary, a girl may feel a slight twinge in one side of her lower abdomen. As the uterus lining builds up, she may feel

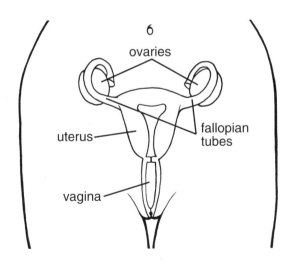

Male and Female

When God made males and females, He created some parts that are alike and others that are different. Mark the changes that happen only to females with an *F*. Mark the changes that happen only to males with an *M*. Write *B* if the change occurs in both male and female.

___ 1. Testosterone levels increase and change begins.

___ 2. Estrogen levels increase and change begins.

___ 3. The voice deepens.

___ 4. Facial hair grows coarse and thick.

___ 5. Pubic hair develops.

___ 6. Shoulders become broader.

___ 7. The pelvic area expands making hips broader.

___ 8. Muscular development occurs.

___ 9. A softer, rounder shape develops.

___ 10. Weight gain is noticed.

___ 11. Physical growth begins around ten years of age and stops around sixteen.

___ 12. Physical growth begins around twelve years of age and stops around twenty.

Look for the answers in "Let's Get Physical!" (beginning on page 6). Then, check your answers at the end of this heavy or bloated. Sometimes her back hurts. Hormones may also make her feel down or slightly depressed. All of these symptoms are normal. In fact, doctors call this Premenstrual Syndrome or PMS.

During the first day of menstrual flow, a girl may feel some cramping. Cramps usually last a few hours. Intense or extended cramps should be reported to a doctor. On an average the menstrual flow lasts five to seven days. It becomes lighter toward the end of the period. During menstruation a girl wears a pad to protect her clothing. Some girls also wear special tubes of absorbent cotton called tampons.

At first, a girl's menstruation cycle may be irregular. That is because her body is adjusting to this new, major event. Gradually a regular cycle will develop. Early in a girl's menstruation, eggs are not mature enough to become fertilized. There is no way of knowing, however, when a girl produces mature eggs. Contrary to a popular myth, a female can become pregnant during any part of her cycle, including menstruation. *(Number 6 is false.)*

The female hormone estrogen also stimulates other kinds of growth. *Breast* development is one of the first signs of puberty in a female. Although the breasts are not actually sex organs, they contain sensitive nerve endings in the nipples that add to sexual arousal. Breast growth occurs over a period of two or three years. During menstruation breasts may swell and become sore.

Shortly after breasts begin to develop, pubic hair grows. Over the next two years hair also grows on arms, legs, and underarms. A girl should discuss with her mother when and how to remove unwanted hair. During puberty a female's body changes shape. Weight gain in girls causes a rounder, softer shape. Her pelvic area broadens. She now has hips and a waist. Girls experience a change in their voices, although it is not as drastic as a boy's voice change.

Those raging hormones affect skin texture. Acne often occurs during times of excess oiliness. Sometimes acne gets worse right before or during menstruation. Stress can also intensify acne.

Like boys, girls experience growth spurts. While girls often begin growing sooner than young men, they also stop growing sooner. A girl usually reaches her adult height by her sixteenth birthday.

Understanding the Sexual Me

Test yourself to see if you know the correct words for sexual growth in boys and girls. Match each word with the correct definition. Answers are italicized in "Let's Get Physical!" (beginning on page 6) and listed at the end of this chapter.

a. hymen
b. cervix
c. labia
d. pituitary gland
e. sperm
f. fallopian tubes
g. uterus
h. vulva

i. scrotum
j. testes
k. clitoris
l. ovary
m. hormones
n. glans
o. breasts

p. semen
q. vagina
r. penis
s. prostate
t. urethra
u. egg
v. seminal vesicle

_____ 1. The male sex organ.

_____ 2. The visible part of the female sex organs.

_____ 3. The outer lips that protect the female's sex organ.

_____ 4. The female reproductive cell.

_____ 5. A pear-shaped muscle designed to nourish a developing fetus; also called the womb.

_____ 6. The sensitive part of the penis.

_____ 7. The male reproductive cell.

_____ 8. Narrow passageways between the ovaries and the uterus.

_____ 9. One of two almond-shaped organs located on either side of the uterus; the place where immature eggs are stored.

____ 10. A sac-like membrane that holds the testicles.

____ 11. The fluid expelled during ejaculation.

____ 12. Two organs on either side of the prostate used to make semen.

____ 13. The narrow tube that carries urine out of the bladder in both males and females.

____ 14. Two organs that produce sperm.

____ 15. Not a sex organ, but increases sexual arousal when stimulated.

____ 16. Estrogen, progesterone, and testosterone.

____ 17. A small knob-like organ with no reproductive function; brings pleasurable sensations during sex arousal.

____ 18. The entrance to the uterus from the vagina.

____ 19. The main gland in the body that controls sexual growth and sexual cycles.

____ 20. A gland located behind the bladder that produces semen.

____ 21. The female's primary sex organ.

____ 22. A thin, flexible membrane that may cover the opening of the vagina prior to the first sexual intercourse.

I Wish Someone Would Tell Me

Knowing about the sex organs and how they function does not mean you know all the answers about sexuality. It's OK to still have questions about what is happening to your body. Write three of your questions in the space that follows.

1.

2.

3.

Look for possible answers as you read about common misconceptions and questions others ask.

▲ *I wish someone would tell me why adults cannot discuss sex without being embarrassed.*

There are several reasons why some people feel uncomfortable with the topic. Many object to open discussions of a subject that is so private and intimate. Some may fear showing their ignorance while friends appear to know everything. Others may be concerned that people will think they are sex maniacs if they talk about sex. Sometimes a person's prejudices and upbringing complicate the situation.

Maybe you do not feel comfortable talking about sex. That's normal. Your sexual development is very personal. Hopefully this book will help you answer some of your questions. If not, find an adult friend and share your questions with that person. Ask a parent, a close relative, a friendly neighbor, a Sunday School teacher, or your minister of youth.

▲ *I wish someone would tell me why my breasts are growing bigger, too. I didn't think this happened to guys.*

About 80 percent of the young men going through puberty experience a temporary swelling in their breasts. The breasts might become sore or sensitive. This is caused by the small amount of estrogen in a man's body. Usually the condition corrects itself over a brief period of time. If breasts remain large, it can be medically corrected with hormone treatment.

▲ *I wish someone would tell me about wet dreams. It's so embarrassing.*

Wet dreams, or nocturnal emissions, occur while a young man is asleep. It is a spontaneous ejaculation. This ejaculation may be triggered by a sexual dream. This occasional event is the body's normal way of dealing with sperm buildup.

▲ *I wish someone would tell me why I get an erection at the most inconvenient times.*

The Right Word

Ejaculation—The rapid spurt of semen and sperm from the penis after sexual stimulation, usually during orgasm.

Foreplay—All activity that sexually arouses a couple in such a way that it leads to sexual intercourse.

Masturbation—The stimulation of the sex organs by hand to produce sexually pleasurable feelings.

Menarche—The first time a girl menstruates.

Orgasm—The intense sensation that occurs at the peak of sexual stimulation. Prior to orgasm the heart beats rapidly, blood pressure rises, rapid breathing occurs, and muscles tighten. There is no awareness of time or place. At the point of climax involuntary muscles contract involuntarily. A quiet, relaxed feeling follows.

Sex—A broad term for defining gender or actions. It is used to define gender (What is your sex—male or female?). It is also used as a short way of saying sexual intercourse.

Sexuality—The sexual nature of each person. Sexuality looks at all that pertains to a person's life, not just sexual activities. Each male and female has specific physical characteristics and sexual functions. Sexuality also determines what roles to accept and how to relate to others. *(Number 10 is false.)*

Sexual Intercourse—The insertion of the penis into the vagina; also called coitus.

It is not unusual for a boy to feel he lacks control of his penis. Of course, it happens at the worst time when everyone appears to be watching.

Several different activities can bring about a spontaneous erection. For example, seeing a pretty girl or having sexual thoughts can be stimulating. In addition, these also cause erections: tension and stress; fright; anger; friction from clothing; the smell of perfume; and accidentally rubbing against someone.

Although girls do not have erections, they can also feel sexually stimulated. Watching a romantic love scene, reading a sexy story, or seeing that special guy all cause some girls to feel sexual desire. This is normal.

▲ *I wish someone had told me that menstruation is a positive event, not a negative one.*

A girl's attitude towards menstruation makes a difference in handling this monthly experience. Some girls think of menstruation as a bother. They may even call it *the plague.* Others feel good knowing that their bodies are working correctly. For others, it is a monthly reminder of their unique status as a female.

Occasionally someone may say to you, "Your menstrual cycle means you are now a woman." Be careful of that attitude. As a developing female, you are already a woman. You will continue to be a woman even when your periods stop in middle age. Menstruation does not determine your femininity.

This is an exciting time in your body's development. As a female you are now equipped for sexual activity and carrying a baby. The key is discovering how to use your new body responsibly.

▲ *I wish someone would tell me that the size of my penis doesn't affect my masculinity.*

▲ *I wish someone would tell me that the size of my breasts doesn't affect my femininity.*

A major goal in growing up is to accept and take care of the body God has given you. Many teenagers, however, compare their bodies to those of their friends.

Unfortunately, society proclaims a *bigger is better* attitude. This is not true.

The size and shape of the penis is not related to race, masculinity, or ability. When the penis is soft, it may differ in size when compared to others. These differences usually disappear, however, during erection. Because the penis is not a muscle, it will not grow larger with frequent erections or shrink from lack of use.

Breast size varies dramatically among females. Actually, girls with large, heavy breasts often have trouble fitting into clothes. The weight of large breasts can also make them very uncomfortable. One doctor suggests that smaller breasts may be better because each breast contains a certain number of nerve endings in the nipple, which are more localized and more sensitive in smaller breasts.

▲ *I wish someone would tell me about toxic shock syndrome.*

Toxic shock syndrome is a serious disease. It is caused by the abnormal growth of bacteria in tampons. Tampons are absorbent tubes of cotton fibers worn inside the vagina during menstruation. Many women wear tampons. Tampons are not the problem; how they are used is the problem.

To prevent toxic shock syndrome change tampons at least every four to six hours. Do not wear tampons all during menstruation. As the flow decreases, use pads designed for light days.

Know the symptoms of toxic shock syndrome. Report a high fever, vomiting, and diarrhea during menstruation to your parents, and see a doctor immediately. Girls die of toxic shock syndrome if it goes untreated.

▲ *I wish someone would tell me about masturbation.*

Masturbation is the stimulation of the sexually sensitive body parts in order to gain sexual pleasure. It is usually done alone. Years ago people thought masturbation caused warts or led to insanity. Neither is true.

Adults, as well as teenagers, have mixed feelings about this sexual activity. Some people believe masturbation is a normal part of growing up as you learn about your body and how it functions. Others support masturbation as a way to release sexual tension without becoming involved in sexual intercourse. Still others believe that a person should control all sexual impulses until marriage.

The Bible contains no explicit references to masturbation. *(Number 7 is false.)* Each person decides about masturbation based on principles and values. Some who feel masturbation is wrong do so based on their understanding of biblical principles such as those found in Philippians 4:8. That means you have to decide how you feel about it based on your knowledge of other parts of the Bible. Masturbation is neither right nor wrong unless it becomes an obsession, or makes the participant feel uncomfortable or embarrassed. It becomes completely wrong, however, if the act dominates a person's life. Masturbation is a self-pleasuring act. A person who masturbates seeks self-pleasure rather than looking for ways to give to others.

This is an area where you may want to talk to a parent or a trusted adult friend. This issue should be part of your prayer life.

▲ *I wish someone would tell me why I sometimes feel out of control.*

Have you ever started to laugh for no reason and could not stop? Do you cry, even during a happy event? Do you feel depressed on some days and ready to go on others? All that is normal.

Right now your body requires large doses of hormones. You have already seen the role of hormones in the development of your sex organs and other body parts. Hormones also influence your moods and feelings. There will be days when you will feel high as a kite, tense, and ready to spring into action. Laughing, talking, and acting crazy seem natural. At other times, you will feel sad and exhausted. Crying and anger may occur during this

20

time. The hormone level in your body makes a difference in your moods. *(Number 8 is true.)*

As you grow older your hormone level stabilizes. You will have more days when you feel even, not sky high or in a deep depression. As you mature you will also learn to control your emotions better.

Did these answer your questions? OK. Now consider your feelings about your sexuality. Complete these sentences to express those feelings.

The part about my body I still don't understand is. . .

I feel better knowing. . .

The Sexual Scene

You have already seen that you are in the process of becoming an adult. As you can see, it's a complex process. How you feel toward the opposite sex is a part of your sexual growth. The physical dimension of your sexual development is only one part; spiritual, social, and emotional dimensions also play a part.

Gradually you will feel comfortable with both male and female friends. One day, however, you will look at a friend of the opposite sex differently. Every time you see that person your heart may beat faster. Your hands may sweat and turn cold. Your stomach may somersault around your insides. A touch by this person may send electric jolts through your body. Finally, you'll get up enough nerve to hold hands.

These are the first sexual feelings towards another person. Relating to the opposite sex involves a whole range of sexual expressions. Each level of sexual expression moves a person physically and emotionally towards sexual intercourse, which the Bible teaches should be reserved for the marriage relationship (Gen. 2:18-24).

Hugs and kisses quickly follow holding hands. Kissing can be a problem if you are just starting out. The first time I kissed a guy, I landed a wet smacker under his left eye. His kiss zeroed in somewhere around my chin.

Try these pointers. Keep your eyes open until you know where your kiss is going to land. Then close your eyes to prevent a cross-eyed view of the other person's nose. Tilt your head to one side so noses do not collide. If you or the other person is wearing braces, do not press too hard. Kissing is supposed to be pleasant, not dangerous.

Necking refers to kisses and hugs that go on for a long time. Touching one another feels special, too. Appropriate touching includes having an arm around the other's shoulders or waist. Placing a hand on the other person's hips or legs are examples of inappropriate touching. This type of touching quickly results in sexual arousal, especially in boys.

Deep kissing also sexually arouses a couple. This is more than a pleasant date kiss or even a good-night kiss. In deep kissing, or French kissing, one person places a tongue in the other person's mouth. Within marriage, deep kissing is foreplay to sexual intercourse.

Petting is often defined as touching sexually sensitive features below the neck. Light petting involves caressing the other person's body through clothing. Stroking a girl's breasts or touching one another's genitals creates sexual stimulation even through clothing. Heavy petting moves into fondling sexually sensitive areas under clothing or without clothing.

Combined with prolonged kissing, any kind of petting propels a couple into deep sexual desire. These exciting sensations make it difficult to stop. Many teenagers cannot control their actions from this point.

This strong passion, called foreplay, leads naturally to sexual intercourse. If a couple does stop, they will feel

What If . . .

Look at life from a different point of view. Decide how you would react in these *What If* situations.

1. *What if* you woke up one day to find yourself completely grown? Your body was exactly the way it would be when you turn twenty-one. How would you feel? What would you miss about growing up gradually?

2. *What if* you could spend one week as either a child or an adult? Which would you choose? What age would you be? Why?

3. *What if* your best friend's body developed quicker than yours? You still looked like a child. How would you feel? What would you do? What if the reverse was true? How could you help your friend accept slower development?

4. *What if* you could change any feature about your sexual growth? What would you change? Why?

5. *What if* boys and girls got married when they turned thirteen? How would you feel about that? What would you like? What would you dislike?

tension and conflict. To go this far every time they are together actually creates problems. Gradually a couple will desire more physical contact while feeling more and more guilty.

Lying down together, removing some or all clothing,

and touching the other person's genitals continues sexual stimulation. Intense arousal causes blood to pour into sexual organs. The penis and vulva secrete fluids to make entry of the penis into the vagina easier. Breathing becomes faster. Blood pressures rise. The mind forgets about time and place. At this point the body is prepared for sexual intercourse.

Within marriage, sexual intercourse is the most intimate form of communication. *(Number 9 is true.)* Together two people share something with one another that they share with no one else in the world! God made male and female to fit together in this unique way. Within marriage sexual intercourse provides a beautiful, personal way to please the person you love the most. Outside of marriage, sexual intercourse can produce guilt, confusion, and frustration because it is outside of God's plan.

Many teenagers believe they can control their actions. They allow themselves to become sexually aroused over and over. Even though a couple may not have sexual intercourse, intense sexual behavior is just as wrong outside of marriage. Sexual game-playing actually uses the other person. Instead of giving, it is taking; instead of loving, it is abusing.

Compare 1 Thessalonians 4:3-7 in your translation of the Bible with these verses from the *New American Standard Bible.*

For this is the will of God, your sanctification; that is, that you abstain from sexual immorality; that each of you know how to possess his own vessel in sanctification and honor, not in lustful passion, like the Gentiles who do not know God; and that no man transgress and defraud his brother in the matter because the Lord is the avenger in all these things, just as we also told you before and solemnly warned you. For God has not called us for the purpose of impurity, but in sanctification (1 Thess. 4:3-7).

These definitions will help you understand this passage. *Sanctification* is the process of being holy or set apart. *Sexual immorality* involves any sexual activity outside of marriage.

Use these verses to answer these questions.

1. Which verse urges you to avoid sexual immorality?

2. Which verse reminds you to act differently than someone who does not know God?

3. Which verse states that you should not harm another sexually by leading them on?

4. Which verse calls you to purity?

Now it's your turn. Where would you draw the line? Draw a *squiggly* line after the sexual activity that you think is OK under God's call for purity. Draw a *straight* line after the sexual activity to indicate how far you think you can go.

- **looking at the opposite sex**
- **hanging around another person**
- **holding hands**
- **hugging**
- **occasional kissing**
- **appropriate touching**
- **frequent kissing**
- **prolonged kissing and hugging (necking)**
- **deep kissing (French kissing)**
- **light petting (through clothing)**
- **heavy petting (under clothing)**
- **lying down together**
- **removing some clothing**
- **removing all clothing**
- **touching another's genitals**
- **mutual masturbation**
- **sexual intercourse**

It is important for you to decide where to draw the line before you are actually involved in sexual activity. If you allow yourself to become comfortable with sexual activity, you usually end up going further than you meant to. Sexual arousal is addictive; each time you want a little more.

No P.D.A.

Behavior has to be appropriate for the situation. During school, in church or Bible study, and on Christian-related activities, public displays of affection (P.D.A.) are inappropriate.

You may want to show off your new boyfriend or girlfriend. Public displays of affection embarrass others. They do not want to see the two of you kissing and hugging. Inappropriate public affection makes the two of you look silly, especially if you change boyfriends or girlfriends frequently.

Flirting

Light flirting, such as writing notes to one another, winking, smiling, and talking to each other on the phone, is acceptable. This type of flirting helps you learn how to communicate with the opposite sex. This flirting is innocent.

Flirting becomes harmful when it teases another person by implied sexual advances. A flirt acts surprised when the other person responds to these sexual advances. Revealing clothing is a subtle way of flirting. Body language, like running your tongue over your lips or bumping into the other person, is also a way of flirting that can be harmful. This type of behavior turns on another person sexually, without intending to carry out sexual activity. Neither boys nor girls like to be teased. Some people react to flirting with anger or abuse. Be careful how you flirt, and what messages you send out. Someone may think you are serious.

Some-Body:
Construction in Progress

What do you see in the mirror? Ears that are too big? A mouth that is bigger than your face? Hair that sticks out everywhere?

Look at your body. How do you feel about your chest area? Are you happy with your height and weight? Do the sexual changes in your body please or embarrass you? Does your new body confuse you?

This is normal. You are a *body under construction.* While construction is taking place, people notice the mess. They do not see the beauty of the building until it is complete. You are not complete; God has not finished with you inside or out. In many ways you are just beginning. Gradually you will become more comfortable with your body. You'll learn how to style your hair so it looks attractive. You'll learn how to walk without falling over your feet. You will learn how to like yourself. Most people grow better looking as they get older. You will, too. You'll also feel better about yourself.

Your physical growth is just part of the story. You are also developing emotionally, mentally, and spiritually. Growing up is the process of learning what to do and when. You will learn how to make smart decisions, sometimes by making poor decisions and having to live with the consequences. You will learn what you can and cannot do. You will learn how to take responsibility for your actions.

God made each person different. No one is an exact copy of any other person. You have abilities and talents that make you special. You also have limitations.

Think about you. Be honest as you write the following letter to yourself.

Dear _____,

    At this time, I am _____ (write in your age). During the last six months, these things have changed about my body:

    Most of my friends have / have not (circle one) experienced these same changes. That makes me feel . . .

Presently, I see these positive qualities in myself. (Check those that apply.)

- ❏ friendly
- ❏ accepting of self
- ❏ adventuresome
- ❏ open
- ❏ encourager
- ❏ honest
- ❏ tuned in to God
- ❏ caring
- ❏ patient
- ❏ accepting of others
- ❏ helper
- ❏ loving

The way I feel about my positive qualities is . . .

I think my main limitation is (check one):

- ❏ conceit
- ❏ critical of self
- ❏ critical of others
- ❏ deceitful
- ❏ disruptive
- ❏ confusion about God

- ❏ self-centeredness
- ❏ thoughtlessness
- ❏ spitefulness
- ❏ won't follow God
- ❏ rebellious
- ❏ seeks revenge

The way I feel about my limitation is . . .

In the future, I hope these things will happen to me (check those that apply):

- ❏ like myself
- ❏ be popular
- ❏ be different
- ❏ date regularly
- ❏ get married
- ❏ make a good friend
- ❏ feel comfortable with my body
- ❏ feel comfortable around others
- ❏ become a good friend
- ❏ do something to get others' attention
- ❏ remain pure until marriage
- ❏ improve my relationship to God
- ❏ have a better relationship with my parents

In order to reach these goals, I will have to . . .

In six months reread this letter. See which attitudes change. Reevaluate your positive and negative qualities. Decide which future goals you are reaching.

Remember you are becoming an adult. You don't have all the answers right now. Those answers will come over the next few years as you make mistakes, look for new ways to improve, and accept yourself. In a couple of years, it would be fun to read this letter again. You may be really surprised how much you have grown!

Answers to "Male and Female" (page 12)
1. M; 2. F; 3. M; 4. M; 5. B; 6. M; 7. F; 8. M; 9. F; 10. B; 11. F; 12. M

Answers to "Understanding the Sexual Me" (page 14)
1. r. penis; 2. h. vulva; 3. c. labia; 4. u. egg; 5. g. uterus; 6. n. glans; 7. e. sperm; 8. f. fallopian tubes; 9. l. ovary; 10. i. scrotum; 11. p. semen; 12. v. seminal vesicle; 13. t. urethra; 14. j. testes; 15. o. breasts; 16. m. hormones; 17. k. clitoris; 18. b. cervix; 19. d. pituitary; 20. s. prostate; 21. g. vagina; 22. a. hymen

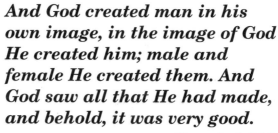

CHAPTER 2

Male and Female— Isn't It Great?

And God created man in his own image, in the image of God He created him; male and female He created them. And God saw all that He had made, and behold, it was very good.

Genesis 1:27,31

The fact that you are a male or a female makes you sexually unique. You studied the physical side of sexuality in Chapter 1. In this chapter you will discover other differences in boys and girls.

First, take the following true-false test. Again look for the answers as you read this chapter.

_____ 1. Your sexuality influences all areas of your life.

_____ 2. Boys and girls are basically the same except for their physical differences.

_____ 3. Because we are all humans, it's easy to understand the opposite sex.

_____ 4. The way you feel about yourself affects the way you act around other people.

_____ 5. Your family impacts your idea of sex.

_____ 6. A girl can become sexually aroused by kissing a boy.

_____ 7. Finding a marriage partner is the major reason that young teenagers date.

_____ 8. A good personality is the most important thing girls want in a boyfriend.

_____ 9. The most important thing boys want in a girlfriend is that she have a great body.

_____ 10. A healthy reason to date is to have fun.

Who Am I Sexually?

By itself this question is not difficult to answer. Your sexuality was determined at conception when the male sperm fertilized the female egg. On the day you were born, your family announced to the world, "We have a boy!" or "It's a girl!" When someone says, "Boys on this side of the room; girls on the other side," you know where to stand. That's the physical side of sexuality.

The mental, emotional, and social sides of sexuality define how you think about yourself and how you relate to others. *(Number 1 is true.)* During adolescence many times you will ask yourself, *Who am I?* In finding out that answer, you learn more about your sexuality.

A teenager wants answers to these questions: How do I fit society's idea of a male or female? How do I want to think and act around guys/gals? What does God expect of me as a male or female? God created sexuality. That creation is recorded in two chapters—Genesis 1:26-28 and 2:18-23. In the second chapter, man was so excited about the creation of woman that he burst into song (v. 23)!

At creation God made man and woman in His own image. Being made in God's image placed these creations over all other life. Animals act on instinct. People can reason and make choices. Animals have limited communications. People can communicate with one another and with God. Working on a biological time clock animals use sex to reproduce. People choose to have sexual relations, sometimes for reasons other than reproduction.

God made each sex equal, but different. *(Number 2 is false.)* The opposite sex is really opposite. Most noticeable are the physical differences. But scientists also have noted the psychological and emotional differences.

Your sexual development began within your family. Boys primarily learn how to act like a man from their fathers; girls from their mothers. *(Number 5 is true.)* As you grow, you also look at others and decide whether to follow the roles they model.

The personal values you adopt during your life determine how you use your sexuality. Some people use their

The Right Word

These words appear in this chapter's Scripture.

Adultery—Sexual intercourse between a married person and someone who is not his or her mate.

Cleave—Two opposite definitions: (1) to cling to or adhere; (2) to divide or split apart. Taken from Genesis 2:24, the first definition is the one intended.

Fornication—Sexual intercourse between two unmarried people.

God's Image—A reflection of the nature of God; being able to communicate with God; having the ability to reason and make choices.

sexuality to gain money, popularity, or power. Others use their sexuality to play on people's emotions and sympathies. Still others recognize the responsibilities that go with sex.

Match up these major points about you as a sexual being with one of these Bible passages:

a. Proverbs 22:6
b. Genesis 2:18,21-23
c. Genesis 1:27,31a
d. Deuteronomy 6:4-7
e. Psalm 8:5.

_____ 1. God made man and woman as companions, equal, but not identical.
_____ 2. God was pleased with His creation of female and male.
_____ 3. People reflect the glory and majesty of God.
_____ 4. The family begins the task of teaching their children how to relate to God and others.
_____ 5. A healthy family models faith and values for their children to use in the future.

Look for the answers at the end of Chapter 2.

The Sex Part of Sexuality

In addition to making males and females, God also created sexual intercourse. As God's invention, sexual intercourse is not evil. God intended this incredible gift for pleasure, for communication, and for reproduction within the marriage relationship.

At creation God saw man was lonely. He created woman as a companion and a helper. Male and female fit together to form a whole in sexual intercourse. Unlike any other relationship in life, sex allows two people to share in deeply personal ways.

Like other gifts from God, sex must be used properly. Responsible sex comes within the commitment of marriage. God made that clear at creation (Gen. 2:24).

Marriage is the public act that identifies a private commitment. Two people promise to live together as life-long companions. Marriage does not wipe away a person's identity. Instead, each person grows. Two people leave behind their self-centered ways and work to give each other the best.

God also established sexual intercourse as the way for people to reproduce. He encouraged them to "be fruitful and multiply" (Gen. 1:28).

Sex is more than a physical act needed for reproduction, however. Animals have sex by biological instinct. People do not need to act like animals. In marriage, they choose their sex partner. They can express care, concern, feelings, and commitment to their mates. They can trust each other to want the best for the relationship. Animals operate on the basic principle of if it feels good, do it. Fortunately, sex within marriage provides not only pleasure, but a total giving up of selfishness.

The way you feel about sex begins with what you see at home. In a healthy home, parents model love and respect for one another. Children see how the commitment of marriage is kept. When parents relate positively to one another, their children learn healthy ways to relate to the opposite sex. If parents relate in a harmful way, children learn not to trust the opposite sex.

Today many teenagers have less than perfect home situations. Some homes have only one parent. Others blend two families in remarriage. A few parents sexually or physically abuse their children. Some parents look for sex outside of marriage. If you live in a family that has unhealthy habits, talk to an adult Christian friend. You need help in sorting out healthy and unhealthy ways to relate to the opposite sex. You do not need to act like parents who have unhealthy habits. God gave you a brain. Make the decisions about your sexuality based on

God's Word that are best for you.

Match these statements about sex with one of the following Bible passages.

a. Hebrews 13:4
b. 1 Corinthians 6:15-20
c. Genesis 1:28
d. Proverbs 5:18-19
e. Genesis 2:24

____ 1. God made male and female to fit together in a unique way through sexual intercourse.
____ 2. You are responsible for the healthy use of your body and your sexuality.
____ 3. God's gift of sexual intercourse takes place within marriage.
____ 4. Sexual intercourse should express love.
____ 5. One purpose of sexual intercourse is to make babies.

The answers are at the end of Chapter 2.

If Wishes Came True

It takes time and effort to figure out how to get along with the opposite sex. Understanding one another is not easy—ever! *(Number 3 is false.)*

For example, how you feel about yourself makes a difference in how others feel about you. When Corey was in the eighth grade, he struggled with balancing the person others wanted him to be and the person he wanted to be. After much thought, he said, "When I like me, others like me, too. When I don't like me, no one else likes me." He was right. *(Number 4 is true.)*

The more you know about the opposite sex, the more understanding you gain. Here are a few things that young men and women wish the other sex knew.

What Young Men Wish Young Women Knew About Them

- "Don't condemn me when I want to hang around with other guys," Robert stated emphatically. "Sure I like girls. But right now girls are not the most important thing in my life. I would rather play basketball or go to a pro game. I wish the girls I know would stop thinking I'm a freak just because I won't talk to them all the time."

- "I hate it when girls talk about us to their girlfriends," complained Shawn. "They act like we don't have any feelings. They laugh at us. They make jokes about us. It's not fair to judge me now. I can't help it if my face looks like *zit city*. I already feel yucky about myself. Why do they have to make it even worse?"

- "I'm sensitive, too. I just don't know how to show it." Jose hesitated before continuing, "Oh, I know guys are supposed to be strong and not show emotion. That doesn't mean I'm not torn up inside. I wish I could cry, too. It's hard for me to show feelings of concern when I'm trying to be tough."

- "Girls don't realize how their clothing and their actions turn me on," Randall disclosed. "Some girls hug me or sit on my lap. Wow! That makes me uncomfortable. I wish I could control my body, but it's like supercharged. I look at a girl wearing a tight sweater or a tiny bathing suit. *Zap! Boing!* My body goes crazy. I don't think girls realize how their innocent actions set off a guy. Some boys can handle it; not me. That's why I walk away when a girl hugs everyone. I just can't take it."

What Young Women Wish Young Men Knew About Them

- "Guys think they're the only ones who get nervous. Well, I get nervous, too," Gayle solemnly tried to explain. "Just because I look grown up, doesn't mean I know what to do or say with boys. Sometimes I get my words mixed up. What's worse, I can't think of anything to say. My friends say relax and do what comes naturally. Nothing comes naturally. I feel so awkward."

- "I get sexual feelings, too," Kathi shared with surprise. "I was with this older boy I really like. He was kissing me, and I was really getting turned on. Gosh, that scared me! I'm a Christian. I thought I'd be able to handle this. Sure it's fun to flirt with guys, but I was surprised by the desire I had." *(Number 6 is true.)*
- "It hurts when a boy brags about me to the other boys," Connie added. "And some boys even make up stuff. That ruins your reputation. Why do they brag to one another? I wish I could find a boy who liked me enough to keep quiet."

Being Friends with the Opposite Sex

You aren't born knowing how to get along with people. You learn that behavior, first from your parents, and later from your friends. Just as you are physically growing, you are also developing in your social skills.

Test your relationship skills. Circle one answer under each statement. Total your points according to the answer box on page 42.

1. Most of the time, I:
   a. like the way I look and act.
   b. want to trade bodies with someone else.
   c. feel like a worm.
   d. realize I'll be OK one day.
2. The best way to learn how to get along with the opposite sex is to:
   a. copy the actions of an older friend, brother, or sister.
   b. do like they do in the movies.

   c. ask my parents for advice.

   d. spend time in a healthy way with the opposite sex.

3. If one isn't always interested in the opposite sex, he or she is:

   a. weird.

   b. normal.

   c. sexually undeveloped and immature.

   d. a homosexual.

4. If a friend told me to change the way I dress in order to attract the opposite sex, I would:

   a. consider my friend's advice.

   b. tell my friend to get lost.

   c. explain that I am trying to make an individual fashion statement.

   d. evaluate what is wrong or right for me.

5. The opposite sex is most attracted to me because of my:

   a. friendliness.

   b. good body.

   c. sense of humor.

   d. common interests.

6. I am most attracted to someone of the opposite sex because of that person's:

   a. personality.   c. good body.

   b. money.   d. popularity.

7. The easiest subject to talk about with someone of the opposite sex is:

   a. school and teachers.   c. church.

   b. friends.   d. myself.

8. I let someone know I like him or her by:

   a. buying that person a present.

   b. hanging around that person all the time.

   c. cracking jokes and clowning around so that person will notice me.

   d. showing concern or interest in getting to know them.

9. I let someone know I'm not interested in being friends by:
   a. being rude.
   b. being pleasant but firm and saying the person's interesting, but not my type.
   c. telling others how much I hate that person.
   d. laughing in the person's face.

Ideas from the Experts for Getting Along with the Opposite Sex

This expert panel was composed of older teenagers who date. They suggest skills to help you in your same-sex and opposite-sex friendships. Work on one skill at a time until you have mastered the list.

Skill 1—Date when you are ready. It's your call. Do not let friends push you into dating too early.

Skill 2—Fix up the outside. That first impression makes a difference. Take frequent showers. Use deodorant. Keep your hair and nails clean. Wear clean clothes. Others notice when you look terrific.

Skill 3—Work on a positive self-image. Don't just fix up the outside. Work on your attitude, too. Look at life in a positive way. What you don't like, change, including yourself. When Corey realized he didn't like the way he always borrowed money from others, he made a real effort to change.

Skill 4—Hold on to what you know is

right. Once you have decided something is right, don't let others pull you down to their way of thinking.

Skill 5—*Learn to listen.* This one is tough. Don't always talk about yourself. Learn to ask questions that uncover others' interests. Pay attention to what a person says. Others will be flattered that you want to know their thoughts and ideas.

Skill 6—*Help others.* Try to be helpful in many ways. Cheer up someone who is sad. Encourage another in a tough situation.

Skill 7—*Learn to get along.* Watch Christian people who get along with the opposite sex. What do they do? What do they say? Learn from them and be yourself.

Skill 8—*Learn from each experience with the opposite sex.* What worked? What did not? How can the experience be improved next time? What do you need to change? What can you expect next time?

Skill 9—*Smile!* A smile makes you feel better even when you have had a difficult day. A smile invites others to pay attention to you. They want your happiness to rub off on them. Smile all day and see what happens.

Skill 10—*Don't give up.* Figuring out the opposite sex is really tough. You will make mistakes along the way. Keep trying. You've got a lifetime to learn how to get along with others.

10. In all friendships with the opposite sex I try to:
    a. learn something from each relationship.
    b. have fun.
    c. treat the other person like I want to be treated.
    d. get all I can from the other person.

To score yourself, use the following score chart to give yourself points for your answers. Total your points to see the results.

	a	b	c	d		a	b	c	d
1.	3	1	0	3	**6.**	3	0	1	1
2.	2	0	2	3	**7.**	3	3	3	2
3.	0	3	0	0	**8.**	0	2	0	3
4.	2	0	1	3	**9.**	0	3	0	0
5.	3	1	3	3	**10.**	3	2	3	0

26-30 points.—You've got your act together! You enjoy being with friends, and they like being with you. Keep up the good work.

18-25 points.—Work on your friendship skills in the areas where you scored low. Remember, you are becoming an adult; you haven't arrived yet.

3-17 points.—Help! That's what you need, but don't worry. Find instant help in "Ideas From the Experts for Getting Along With The Opposite Sex." Pick out one point to work on each week.

The Dating Game

The best dates start as friendships. Even when you meet someone for the first time and think to yourself, *Wow! That's someone I'd like to date!* you begin with friendship. Right now building healthy friendships with both sexes comes before serious dating. In fact, if you are not ready to date, that's perfectly normal.

Why Date?

Dating helps you mature. Social and communication skills improve as you date and relate to others. At first, dating may feel awkward. The more time you spend with friends of both sexes, the more skilled you will become.

Look over these reasons to date. Mark *H* beside healthy reasons to date. Mark *U* beside unhealthy reasons.

_____ 1. to be like adults
_____ 2. to have fun
_____ 3. to belong to someone
_____ 4. to get to know a person better
_____ 5. to get out of the house
_____ 6. to discover new interests
_____ 7. to impress friends
_____ 8. to get to know someone to whom I'm attracted
_____ 9. to try out sex
_____ 10. to learn to care for another person
_____ 11. to find someone to marry
_____ 12. to learn how to accept another's hang-ups
_____ 13. to make my parents happy
_____ 14. to learn about my likes and dislikes
_____ 15. to find love and acceptance

How did you do? The *even* numbered reasons are the most healthy for your age. *(Number 10 is true.)* Reasons 11 and 15 are more healthy for older teens. Most younger teenagers are not thinking about getting married any time soon. *(Number 7 is false.)*

A main reason to date is to discover what you like and don't like about others. You learn about another's interests. You learn how to put up with another's likes and dislikes. As you date, you eliminate types of people with whom you do not want to spend time. For example, because I felt uncomfortable with a date who drank, I quit dating guys who drank.

My Ideal

Seventeen magazine surveyed 2,000 young people on the qualities they wanted in an ideal boyfriend or girlfriend. The results were published in the October, 1989 issue. Both boys and girls, ages fourteen, said a "good personality" was the the most important trait. *(Number 8 is true; number 9 is false.)* How would your list of ideal traits compare to this survey?

Girls wanted these characteristics in a boyfriend in this order:
1. good personality
2. is considerate of me
3. sense of humor
4. good looks
5. artistic/sensitive
6. intelligence
7. has money

The boys changed the order using the same traits:
1. good personality
2. good looks
3. is considerate of me
4. sense of humor (tied with #3)
5. intelligence
6. artistic/sensitive
7. has money

Some motives for dating are wrong. Dating that uses another person for selfish reasons is always wrong. For example, some teens date just to have a security blanket. Others date to run away from problems at home or

44

school. Some date to experiment with sex. Weak, shallow relationships develop when dating is based on selfish motives.

Dating a Christian allows you to be more relaxed on your dates. You don't have to spend time explaining why you don't want to do certain things. You both should know what is right and wrong.

When Is a Date Not a Date?

Today dating is not restricted to two people going out together. Probably the best type of date for younger adolescents is group dating. On group dates, several boys and girls meet to do something together. There are no couples.

Group dating has several advantages. First, your parents are more likely to let you go out with a group, rather than with one person. Since everyone pays his or her own way, no one gets stuck spending a lot of money. You learn to get along with several different people without being tied down to one person at a time.

The main disadvantage of group dating is that you have to do what the group decides. By working out where to go and what to do you learn to compromise. If you end up going to places you don't like or doing things you don't feel are right, then group dating is no fun. You will have to look for other friends who have interests and values closer to your own.

It is not unusual for early dating experiences to result in new feelings. Crushes and puppy love often occur to teenagers your age. Crushes are usually based on fantasy. You may have a crush on a teacher, an older teenager, or the most popular person at school. Crushes usually last only a few weeks, then end quickly. It is not uncommon to have one crush after another. In puppy love a person swears undying love to another. In reality, the relationship lasts only a brief time. Crushes and puppy love are real emotions. But don't get too hung up by them.

Why Set Guidelines?

Parents are concerned when their teenagers start to date. They have heard all the horror stories about what can go wrong. They know about the pressure you feel to choose different values from those you were taught. They know that society's values clash with Christian values. They also remember the mistakes they made in their early dating.

To protect you, they may establish barriers, instead of boundaries. Barriers are *do's* and *don'ts* set up without your input.

In other instances, they set up boundaries, which establish guidelines to give you freedom. When guidelines are stated, you know your limits. When guidelines are not identified, you don't know how far you can go. If you go too far, you end up being punished for something you did not realize was wrong. Boundaries work best if you are included in setting them.

That is why it is important to work with your parents on a dating contract. Together you and your parents can set up a few guidelines that make everyone happy.

Use the following sample dating contract as a model to record your ideas on dating.

Dating Contract

I think I should be allowed to group date when I'm _____ *(write in age you want to be when you start going out with a group).*

I would like to single date when I turn _____ *(write in appropriate age).*

I consider these to be the best reasons for dating (select from list under "Why Date?" and add your own):
  1.

  2.

3.

I think I should be allowed to go to these places on a date (check all that apply and add your own):

❑ *church-related activities*
❑ *school-sponsored events*
❑ *teen night clubs*
❑ *my house with parents at home*
❑ *my house with no one at home*
❑ *my date's house with parents at home*
❑ *my date's house with no one at home*
❑ *a chaperoned party*
❑ *an unchaperoned party*
❑ *a movie*
❑ *a nice restaurant*
❑ *a fast-food place*
❑ *the mall*
❑ *a rock concert*
❑ _____
❑ _____
❑ _____

I will follow these dating guidelines:

1. *I want to date these types of people:*
   age _____
   interests _____

2. *I want to set a weekend curfew of* _____*; a school night curfew of* _____*.*

3. *I want to go out on* _____ *night during the week and on* _____ *night on the weekend.*

4. I anticipate spending approximately $_____ on a date.

5. I plan to earn the money to spend on a date by _____.

6. I would like to suggest these other related guide-lines:

OK, here's the difficult part. Sit down with your parents. Show them the contract. Talk about each category. Compromise where necessary. If you are already dating, use the contract to gain your parents' support of your dating. Most parents will be pleased with your openness and maturity.

If your parents do not seem interested, or if you hesitate to talk with them, find a Christian, adult friend to help you. Setting up guidelines before you start dating helps avoid misunderstandings later.

A Word of Warning

Dating is a great way to broaden your world. It can be fun, exciting, and challenging. It also can be dangerous. Unfortunately, some people want to harm you. Remember, your body is your responsibility (1 Cor. 6:19-20). God gave you a brain to figure out right and wrong, and the Holy Spirit to guide you.

This is one time to fall back on your parents. If you don't want to go somewhere or do something that the other person does, blame your parents. Tell the person, "Oh, I can't. My folks won't let me." If you need to end an evening early, say "I have to be home by 11:00. That's my curfew." Letting your parents take the blame gets you off the hook. I tell my own teenagers to always blame me if

Would You?

Even though you may not be dating yet, begin now to set standards for future relationships with the opposite sex. Of course, some decisions may change based on circumstances and situations.

Think through each of the following carefully. Consider the consequences—good or bad—of saying *yes* or *no*. Do not sit on the fence by answering *maybe* to more than three. Then write *yes, no,* or *maybe* by the questions.

_____ 1. Would you date someone who is not a Christian?

_____ 2. Would you kiss on a first date?

_____ 3. Would you go on a blind date with someone you've never met?

_____ 4. Would you insist your date meet your parents?

_____ 5. Would you let your date pay your way on a date?

_____ 6. Would you pay your own way on a date?

_____ 7. Would you talk about your date afterward with your friends?

_____ 8. Would you date someone more than two years older than you?

_____ 9. Would you date someone more than two years younger than you?

_____ 10. Would you date someone

it gets them out of a tight situation.

One more word of warning, especially to girls. Date rape is a very real problem, mainly on college campuses and for older girls. But date rape can happen to any female who is dating.

Rape is any sex act that you are forced to do without your consent. Rape is an act of violence, not of love or concern. Sex is not payment for a date. You do not owe a boy any kind of sex for dating you.

One way to prevent date rape is to be cautious. Stay out of empty buildings, including your home if no one is home. Do not sit in a parked car in an isolated place. Know the person you are dating before you go out with him. Do not lead a fellow on with sexual flirting.

Smart girls carry change so they can call home. This is another area you need to talk about with your parents before you start dating. Parents want to know about a younger teen's dating activities. A concerned and responsible parent can be a counselor and friend to you during early dating experiences.

This chapter gives you a lot to think about. Let's summarize the high points:

• You are in the process of discovering how sexuality fits into your life.

• God made you a sexual being. He created the sex act and wants you to enjoy it in the marriage relationship. He called both of these good.

• It takes time and effort to learn how to get along with the opposite sex.

• Dating is a pleasant way of learning how to relate to the opposite sex.

• Your parents can be a helpful part of your initial dating experiences, if you will let them.

Answers for "Who Am I Sexually" (page 34)
1. b; 2. c; 3. e; 4. d; 5. a.

Answers for "The Sex Part of Sexuality" (page 36)
1. e; 2. b; 3. a; 4. d; 5. c.

CHAPTER 3

You're in Charge

Whatever is true, whatever is honorable, whatever is right, whatever is pure, whatever is lovely, whatever is of good repute, if there is any excellence and if anything worthy of praise, let your mind dwell on these things.

Philippians 4:8

Peer pressure. Teenagers deny its power over them. Parents dread its deadly hold on their kids. Advertisers use it to promote the latest fashion, food, or fun. Whether you realize it or not, you make life-changing decisions based on pressure from your friends.

Both boys and girls want you to go along with their ideas. Smart teenagers are not easily misled. For example, how would you answer these lines concerning sexual pressure from a boyfriend or girlfriend?

If you really love me, . . .

You don't want to be the only virgin in school, do you?

Come on; it feels so right!

If you won't, I'll find someone else who will.

What are you afraid of? No one will ever know.

You can control your body. You do not need to give in to the pressure from one person or the crowd. God gave you a brain, as well as a body. Learn how to use both responsibly. In this chapter discover how to say no and mean it.

First, test your knowledge about the realities of premarital sex by marking the following statements with *true* or *false*. Then look for the correct answers in this chapter.

_____ 1. The words *I love you* often mean something different to boys than they do to girls.

_____ 2. Lust is merely thinking sexual thoughts.

_____ 3. The first sexual encounter for younger teenagers usually occurs in the backseat of a car.

_____ 4. Physical love fulfills all the requirements of true love.

_____ 5. Birth control pills protect a girl from getting a sexually transmitted disease.

_____ 6. The most common sexually transmitted disease among teenagers is AIDS.

_____ 7. All sexually transmitted diseases are incurable.

_____ 8. The *pro-life movement* allows a woman to decide for herself what to do about abortion.

_____ 9. The first time a couple has sexual intercourse is the best it will ever be.

_____ 10. Being sexually active before marriage contributes to being faithful within marriage.

In Love or in Heat?

Along with a new body, you are also discovering new feelings. These new feelings make it difficult to decide what love really is. Let's define love by explaining what it is not.

Sexual arousal is not love. Animals in heat react to sexual arousal in order to reproduce. They mate by instinct, not love. For animals sex is selfish pleasure for a seasonal event. Like animals you can be sexually stimulated without feeling commitment or concern for the other person. Unlike animals you can control your sexual urges.

Movies, advertising, and book fantasies do not always portray true love. Real love survives both the difficult and the happy times of life. Real love is built on communication and trust.

Sometimes love means different things to each sex. Some girls think of *I love you* as a pledge of commitment. Some boys say the words *I love you* and mean them in a physical way. *(Number 1 is true.)*

Love is not the same as sex. Sex is not the same as love. People can have sex without love or commitment. That is not why God invented sex. God did not intend for men and women to act like animals in heat. Which of the statements on the following pages express being in love and which express sex without love? Put a check in the appropriate column and check your answers at the end of the chapter.

In Love			*Sex Without Love*
____	1.	does whatever other person demands	____
____	2.	in love with the idea of love	____
____	3.	trusts the other person	____
____	4.	bases relationship on physical attraction	____

53

_____ 5. knows person's likes and dislikes _____
_____ 6. brags about sex to friends _____
_____ 7. cares about the other person _____
_____ 8. wants to belong to someone _____
_____ 9. shares honest feelings and fears _____

The World's Greatest Lovers

Are you one of the world's greatest lovers? Read 1 Corinthians 13:4-8a, then rate yourself using this report card. If you date, think about your relationship to those you date. If you are not dating, rate yourself in relationships with others. Use school ratings: *A* for excellent; *B* for good; *C* for average; *D* for poor; *F* for failure.

REPORT CARD

Subject	*Grade*
Patient; does not get angry	_____
Kind; concerned; caring	_____
Not jealous	_____
Does not brag about self	_____
Interested in another's	_____

Likes and Dislikes	*Grade*
Gives up selfishness	_____
Not easily irritated	_____
Forgets bad times of the past	_____
Enjoys healthy, Christian activities	_____
Can be trusted	_____
Trusts the other person	_____
Looks for best in other person	_____

_____ 10. shows off for other person   _____
_____ 11. jealous of the other's friends   _____
_____ 12. sees as a temporary relationship   _____
_____ 13. learns from other person   _____
_____ 14. fears losing other person   _____
_____ 15. overlooks another's faults   _____

Six ideas describe love. Nine ideas describe sex without love. Look at "The World's Greatest Lovers" to see what traits best express true love.

In Love or in Lust?

Love and lust also confuse people. In Matthew 5:27-28 Jesus added a warning to the commandment on adultery. He said lust is also a sexual sin.

Lust looks at the opposite sex in a degrading way. Lust fantasizes about how to use another person's body selfishly.

Don't panic. Everyone thinks sexual thoughts; this is not lust. *(Number 2 is false.)* These occasional thoughts differ from the sexual lust that Jesus described. Lust dwells on sexual thoughts and fantasies. These dominate a person's mind and actions.

A person can create lust in others. For example, skimpy clothing may bring on lustful ideas. Pornography plays off lustful fantasies. Proverbs 7:10-27 warns about this lustful teasing.

Look at the different definitions for love in "The Right Word" box on the next page. Love is more than heat or lust. Love exists beyond sex. Love gives. Love grows and changes within a relationship. In marriage two people can ask for love or give love depending on their needs. For example, a husband may have sexual intercourse with his wife if she desires it, even when he is tired.

The Right Word

Infertility/Sterility—The inability to reproduce. *Infertility* produces unhealthy or inadequate eggs or sperm. *Sterility* means the eggs or sperm cannot come together due to damaged reproductive organs.

Licentiousness—Lewd, immoral behavior; often used in the Bible to describe sexual sin.

Love—A broad word related to several ideas: (1) I *love* ice cream (slang); (2) the score of *30-love* (tennis score); (3) I *love* him; he's my brother (natural affection, like that between a mother and child); (4) I'm in *love* (physical attraction, erotic love); (5) I *love* her like a sister (deep, long-lasting friendship); (6) God so *loved* the world *(agape* love that is given even when it is undeserved). True love that occurs between a man and a woman combines the last three examples of love. *(Number 4 is false.)*

Lust—Dwelling on sexual fantasies about using another person's body for sexual satisfaction.

Premarital Sex—Sexual intercourse between partners before marriage.

STD—The abbreviation for sexually transmitted disease. Also called venereal disease or VD. Includes various bacteria and virus infections passed through sexual contact with an infected person.

Virgin; Virginity—Someone who has not had sexual intercourse.

Just Say No and Mean It

Sexual pressure is everywhere. You will see thousands of sex-related activities in movies and on television before you reach adulthood. Music lyrics explicitly promote sex. Friends talk about sex. Your family warns you about the dangers of sex. Your church shouts *don't,* while your body hollers *let's go!* You probably feel bombarded with ideas about sex.

That is not unusual. Sex is a big part of your physical growth. Feeling sexual is normal.

Even before you start dating, you make decisions about the opposite sex. One major decision involves pre-marital sex.

Some young people say *yes* to sexual intercourse before marriage, using these excuses.

I wanted someone to love me.

All my friends are doing it— I didn't want to be left out.

It feels right.

We got caught up at the time.

I thought she wanted it.

I thought he'd leave me if I didn't.

I wanted to get back at Mom and Dad.

I didn't think it would go that far.

I was curious.

Others decide to say *no* and mean it. Their reasons for staying pure vary, too.

I don't believe it's right for me.

My religion says it's wrong.

I'm wroking toward an important goal in my life— nothing will make me miss that goal.

I have other things that keep me busy.

I like myself and know what is right for me.

I want the first time to be with the person I marry.

I don't want to betray my parents' trust.

I decided to stay pure until I'm married.

Three tests can help you decide whether a sexual activity is right or wrong. In fact, these tests can be applied to any action or thought.

• *The Test of Secrecy.*—How would you feel if others knew about your action? (Check out Prov. 15:3.)

• *Test of Universality.*—What if everybody did this activity? (See 1 Cor. 15:33.)

• *The Test of Prayer.*—Can you ask God to bless this activity? Does the action change your relationship to God? (Read 1 John 1:6-7.)

The decision to say *no* and mean it is powerful. You are not alone. Many young men and women choose to be sexually pure. You can't wait, however, until you are in the backseat of a car to make that decision. By then it may be too late!

The most difficult time to say *no* is after you have already said *yes,* even once. You have to know how far you can go and still be in control.

Know Your Limitations

Your physical changes make you feel very sexual. Others notice these changes, too. But this sexual development does not excuse you from learning how to control your thoughts and actions. You learn control by knowing your limitations.

Avoid tempting situations. Many younger teens report that their first sexual encounter occurred in their own homes between 3:00 p.m. and 5:00 p.m. while their parents were at work. *(Number 3 is false.)* Sitting in a parked car in an isolated place is also tempting. Other temptations like watching sexy movies or listening to suggestive music weaken your desire to say *no*.

Emotional moments break down your resistance. Intense, prolonged kisses and caresses move you closer to *yes* and away from *no*. Fatigue breaks down your defenses. Grief makes you want some one to care for you. The fear of losing another also weakens your decision to say *no*. The influence of alcohol or other drugs lowers resistance by blurring moral convictions.

Acting out romantic fantasies appears thrilling at the moment. Do not be surprised, however, if you get caught in a sexual situation.

As you get older, you may gain false self-confidence by thinking you can handle any sexual temptation. You might say *yes* to petting, French kissing, even removing some clothing. At first, these new activities will feel awkward and make you feel guilty. These are warning signs to heed. Gradually, however, you may convince yourself that it's OK. You may even explain to others that what used to be wrong is now right. The more sexually involved you get, the more difficult it is to say *no*. Even the author of Proverbs saw this danger (see Prov. 6:27 and 12:15).

Your body is your responsibility. You can decide to say *no*. Others want you to think, however, that *no* is not necessary. They try to persuade you to say *yes*. They forget to tell you the consequences.

Truth and Consequences

In the 1950s, most girls said *no* to premarital sex to protect their reputations. A sexually active girl was called a tramp.

The 1960s and 1970s brought the sexual revolution and the ideas that virginity was out and that sex for any reason was in.

During the 1980s the dark cloud of consequences spread over the sexual revolution. By the 1990s, society realized that unrestrained sex is not only dangerous, but also deadly. Supporters of the sexual revolution do not like the truth of unrestrained sexual freedom.

The Truth About Sexually Transmitted Diseases

Young people believe they will not get a sexually transmitted disease because they are young. Here are additional false ideas about sexually transmitted diseases.

- You can't get a sexually transmitted disease if the boy pulls out quickly.
- Girls catch things, not macho guys like me.
- Birth control pills protect a female from getting a sexually transmitted disease. *(Number 5 is false.)*
- Washing after intercourse reduces the chance of getting a disease.
- Oral sex is safe.

Sexually transmitted diseases are more likely to occur to those who have more than one sex partner; but if your one sex partner happens to be infected, you too could become infected. Infected people infect others. The World Health Organization estimated that 250 million people worldwide—one in twenty—will contract a sexually transmitted disease.

Sexually transmitted diseases result in recurring pain, infertility or sterility, cancer, blindness, brain damage, and even death. Young adults between the ages of twenty and twenty-four are at greatest risk. Teenagers are the next group at risk.

Sexually transmitted diseases, called STDs, affect more than just the reproductive organs. In the male, infections may spread from the penis and scrotum to the prostate gland and the urethra. Female infections develop in the vagina, uterus, outer lips, vulva, fallopian tubes, and cervix. They may spread to the abdominal cavity, bladder, and urethra. Both sexes can have infections in the mouth, anus, and immune system. When an infection enters the bloodstream, the liver, central nervous system, and skin also become involved.

In addition to physical problems, sexually transmitted diseases cause great psychological and social pain. For example, a person may lose a job because of a STD. Social rejection is another heartache of someone with a STD.

Let's look at the most notorious STDs. Sort out the diseases and their differences by filling out the chart on the following page as you read.

Chlamydia is one of the two most common STDs in the United States. The other is gonorrhea. *(Number 6 is false.)* Reports indicate that between 7 and 40 percent of female teens are infected with chlamydia. Unfortunately, the bacteria that causes chlamydia does not produce clear-cut symptoms. It can cause abdominal pain and nausea in females and painful urination in males, or it may not.

Chlamydia can be treated if diagnosed through a laboratory culture. By the time it is discovered, however, damage to reproductive system may have already occurred. The result can be scar tissue, pelvic pain, and sterility. Chlamydia can also be passed on to newborn babies resulting in pneumonia or eye infections.

Gonorrhea in the male causes a pus-like discharge and painful urination. An infected female may have a pus-like discharge or pelvic pain, but she may not. Left

Sexually Transmitted Diseases

Disease	Symptom	Results	Cure
Chlamydia			
Gonorrhea			
Syphilis			
Human Papilloma Virus (HPV)			
Herpes Simplex Virus (HSV)			
Hepatitis B Virus (HBV)			
Human Immune Deficiency Virus (HIV)			

untreated, gonorrhea enters the blood stream, causing arthritis, heart disease, and meningitis. Babies infected by mothers can become blind. Like chlamydia, gonorrhea must be diagnosed in a laboratory test. Antibiotics cure both diseases. *(Number 7 is false.)* There are cures for some STD's, but others are incurable and some are fatal. Read on.

Syphilis produces a round, crater-like sore that looks painful, but is not. The sores are visible on the penis, but almost impossible to discover in the cervix or vagina. Syphilis can be detected by a blood test. Since 1985 the syphilis rate has jumped to 67 percent among sexually active teens. Many states require such a blood test to get a marriage license. The disease reacts to antibiotics. Untreated syphilis, however, can kill.

The most dangerous STDs are the *H* viruses. These viruses are easily passed through sexual contact. They cause serious health problems and cannot be cured. The *human papilloma virus (HPV)* causes genital warts. More than 30 million cases have been reported. These warts disappear after treatment, but the virus remains in the body. That means genital warts can return at any time. Genital warts have been linked to cancer of the cervix in women and penile cancer in men.

The *herpes simplex virus (HSV)* infects about 20 million people. It is the most common *H* virus. The symptoms are small painful blisters that are visible on the genital areas. The blisters last from one to two weeks. Sometimes the blisters also appear in the mouth or on the fingertips. Some herpes strains respond to medication; others do not. Because there is no cure, these painful blisters can return without warning. This virus is also associated with cervical cancer. Sadly, when passed to the new life during pregnancy, herpes simplex can lead to brain infection and even death in a newborn.

Another *H* virus, *hepatitis B virus (HBV)*, is found in body fluids that include semen, blood, and saliva. Also known as serum hepatitis, this virus has flu-like symptoms. High risk groups include intravenous drug users and homosexuals. Like the other *H* viruses, there is no cure.

What's Wrong with This Picture?

A clean-cut appearance, good manners, and intelligence do not guarantee that a person does not have a sexually transmitted disease. Because of hidden symptoms, the smartest, most acceptable looking person can be a carrier. An infected person can infect another, even though there is no evidence of a sexually transmitted disease.

Teenagers who have sexual intercourse in their early teens tend to have several partners. Each time they change partners, the risk of sexual infection increases. In effect, you have sex with every person who has had sex with your partner.

Consider this question if you get to a point of considering having sex: Are you willing to risk death or disease to have sex with that person?

Religious groups are not the only ones urging sexual purity. Government agencies and medical experts say the only way to stop sexually transmitted disease is for men and women to abstain from sexual intercourse until marriage. If both partners come to the marriage as virgins, and both remain faithful in the marriage, there is no risk of either getting a sexually transmitted disease.

The most infamous *H* virus is the *human immune deficiency virus (HIV),* which leads to AIDS. AIDS is discussed later in this chapter.

Health officials are alarmed by the increasing number of STD cases. Each time an infected person has sexual intercourse with other people the disease is more likely to spread.

Because many symptoms remain hidden, a person may not realize that the disease is present. That person may infect several people before the disease is diagnosed. This nightmare of hidden danger and multiple partners results in ever increasing numbers of infected people.

What's normal? Someone who is not sexually active cannot get a sexually transmitted disease. Normal secretions from the reproductive organs may worry uninformed teens.

Normally a female has menstrual bleeding on a regular cycle. It is also normal to experience a slight discharge of a clear fluid at mid-cycle. The vagina becomes moist during sexual arousal; this is normal. Young men will also have a slight discharge of semen when sexually aroused.

A few diseases of the reproductive organs are not sexually transmitted. These diseases can be treated by a doctor. These symptoms are not normal. A yellow-green, foul-smelling vaginal discharge or a thick, white, cottage-cheese-type discharge is not normal. Vaginal itching is another symptom of a reproductive disease. A girl with these symptoms needs to ask her mother to take her to the doctor. Pelvic pain, other than mild cramps, is another reason to see a doctor.

The Truth About AIDS

The *human immune deficiency virus,* also known as HIV, causes the disease AIDS. This disease attracts great attention from the medical community and the media because of its fatal results. Although AIDS is widely discussed, many people remain confused.

The Facts:

- The AIDS virus kills the body's ability to fight infection. When a person gets sick, the body cannot fight back. Pneumonia and cancer are two diseases that most often kill AIDS patients.
- More than one million people carry the AIDS virus, according to the World Health Organization.
- More people have died of AIDS than died during the Vietnam War.
- The average time from infection to detection is seven to ten years. During that time an infected person can pass on the AIDS virus, even though there are no visible symptoms.
- Teenagers compose 1 percent of the nation's total AIDS cases. Unfortunately, the number of teen cases doubles every fourteen months.
- One in four teenagers is at risk for getting the AIDS virus, according to the Centers for Disease Control. The high risk is due to teenagers freedom-seeking, *I'm indestructible* life-style. Teens often have multiple sexual partners. They frequently do not use condoms. Runaway and homeless teens exchange sex for food, shelter, or drugs.

AIDS was first diagnosed in the United States in 1981 among homosexuals. Since then, AIDS has been detected in all age groups of both sexes. Even babies born to infected mothers contract AIDS. These babies usually live only a short time.

AIDS is sexually passed through body fluids during sexual intercourse, oral sex, and anal sex with someone who is infected. It is contracted by blood transfusions of blood from an HIV positive person. (Today blood donors are screened for HIV.) Also, a hypodermic needle used by an infected person and reused without proper sterilization can spread the virus. (Teenagers sometimes share needles to shoot up drugs, steroids, and even to pierce ears.) In the case of the unborn child, the mother passes the virus to the baby as her body feeds the baby in the womb.

AIDS cannot be spread through casual contact. You cannot get AIDS by talking to a person with AIDS. You cannot get AIDS by touching someone with AIDS. You cannot get AIDS even by using the bathroom after someone who has AIDS.

The good news is that through education people are learning more about AIDS. Education has helped people understand how to relate to people with AIDS. It has also encouraged them to develop careful hygiene habits.

The bad news is that despite intense research there is no cure for AIDS. AIDS kills.

AIDS is detected through a blood test that looks for the virus. If a person tests HIV positive, the virus is present. That person may not have an active case of AIDS, but he or she is at great risk of developing the disease later. An HIV positive person can also pass the virus on to others. Unfortunately, the blood test may turn up negative at an early date, and later come back positive. Doctors and research teams continue to study AIDS. They are trying to figure out how it is passed from one person to another. They search for a cure. They are also hoping to find a vaccine to protect those not currently infected.

Because of the growing number of AIDS cases, you may know someone who has AIDS or who has tested HIV positive. No matter how this person got the disease, you can be an encourager. God cares about that person. You can show God's love by sharing your concern.

Teenagers often think they cannot die. Because of this belief, they go ahead and have premarital sex, most of the time without protection. You must decide. AIDS is deadly. Are you willing to die in order to have sex with a person? The pressure to have premarital sex will be strong, but you need to have standards set in advance. Paul's testimony in Galatians 1:20 is an example for us to follow, "And they glorified God in me." A pure life-style will not only be safe and healthy during the present and in the future but God will be glorified through it.

The Truth About Pregnancy

Becky hunched over in front of me. Tears rolled down her face. "I'm pregnant. What do I do?" She was fourteen years old—still a child herself.

Together we told Becky's parents about her pregnancy. At first her parents were angry. Then they realized the need to help Becky through this time. Because she was young, they did not encourage her to marry the baby's father. Her mom and dad lovingly supported Becky during her pregnancy. When the baby was born, it was placed with a family through an adoption agency.

Becky's family dealt with the difficult problem of teenage pregnancy in a healthy way. Other families do not. Some families, embarrassed by their daughters' behavior, send them to live with relatives. A few parents kick their daughters out of their homes. Still others encourage marriage, even though the baby's parents are young.

Over 1.6 million teenagers become pregnant each year. Of those, 125,000 are 15 years old or younger. The TV program "48 Hours" reported that a young teenager gives birth every 15 hours in a Fairfax, Virginia hospital. Doctors at Grady Hospital in Atlanta, Georgia, each week deliver babies from at least two mothers who are under 15 years of age. Basically, a young teenage girl and her family bear the responsibility for a pregnancy. Most teenage fathers cannot help financially. Teenage fathers are usually not prepared to take on the responsibility of a family. Marriage is one option, but not necessarily the best. Other options, some are not necessarily the best, for a pregnant teenager are:

1. place the baby up for adoption
2. keep the baby, raising it as a single parent
3. keep the baby, letting it be raised by the girl's parents
4. have an abortion

The Truth About Abortion

Induced abortions are a human way of ending a pregnancy. Abortion is not a new idea. Four-thousand-year-old Chinese texts describe abortion techniques. Ancient Greek and Roman civilizations used abortion as a way to control population. Many early Christians objected to abortion just as they did to the pagan practice of abandoning unwanted infants.

In the United States abortions are not only a religious issue, but also a social and political issue. Public debate stirs emotions on both sides. One side urges laws supporting legalized abortions. The other side opposes abortion holding up the sacredness of life.

Pro-choice leaders argue that each woman has the right to decide what happens to her body. They oppose government regulations against abortion. They want government money to be used for abortions.

The *pro-life* group believes that life begins at conception—at the time when the sperm fertilizes the egg. They believe each fertilized egg is a creation of God with a soul. This group is against abortion. *(Number 8 is false.)*

Four out of ten pregnant teenagers seek an abortion. These are usually girls from middle and upper-middle income families. Of all abortions performed in the United States each year, 26 percent are done on teenagers. According to the Center for Population Options, only half these girls tell their parents about their abortions.

The father has no legal rights under current law. He can't force the mother to have an abortion. He can't keep her from having an abortion.

There are different types of abortion. A *spontaneous abortion* is called a miscarriage. This usually occurs when there is something physically wrong.

An *induced abortion* is a surgical way of ending a pregnancy. The debate about abortion centers around whether an abortion is ever justified, and if so, when. Some advocates of pro-choice insist that an abortion is justified whenever a pregnant woman decides it is best for her—whatever the reasons. Some pro-life advocates insist that abortion is never justified. Others feel that abortion on demand is wrong; but that under certain extreme conditions, it may be the better of two bad options. Many believe that ending a pregnancy is better than seriously endangering the mother's life. Some consider rape and incest as other extreme conditions that may be considered justification for an abortion.

Abortion is a deceptive issue. Initially for some teenagers an abortion may appear to be the right option for a pregnant teenager. But let's consider the physical, emotional, and spiritual implications.

Physically, abortion increases the risk of infections. Teenage girls are more likely to have pelvic inflammatory disease if they've had an abortion. An abortion on a teenager may cause scar tissue, resulting in sterility. Or the girl may be unable to carry a baby for nine months when she wants to have children later.

Emotional effects may not appear for several months, even years. Some girls never accept their abortions. Memories of their unborn infants haunt them. Others are devastated by the reality of ending a life. Abortions upset some girls so much that they run away from home or attempt suicide.

Abortion remains a controversial subject. The basic issue evolves around the time when a new life becomes human. Christians consider all life precious. God creates life and knows each person from that moment of conception. Many Christians, therefore, consider induced abortion morally wrong.

Look at these Bible verses. Summarize each Scripture in terms of what it says about life.

1. Genesis 1:27

2. Exodus 20:13

3. Job 31:15

4. Job 33:4

5. Psalm 127:3-4

6. Isaiah 44:2

7. Isaiah 49:1

8. Jeremiah 1:4-5

9. Psalm 139:13

You will want to discuss this serious issue with your parents or someone you respect. You will not have to personally face an abortion, however, as long as you remain sexually pure until marriage.

The Truth About Babies

One in ten teenage girls becomes pregnant each year. Sixty percent decide to have their babies. That's 500,000 babies born to teenage mothers each year. Fifteen-year-olds with one child are likely to have a second child before they turn twenty.

One of the biggest problems with teenage mothers is they often drop out of school. With no skills they have to depend on family or welfare for support.

Studies show that the way to break this negative trend of young mothers on welfare is to help them complete high school. Many states provide schools for teenage mothers. Others provide child care while they attend regular classes. This means there must be child care for the 800,000 children of these young mothers.

Many teenage mothers try to raise their children alone. Others live with their parents, placing an additional financial burden on the home.

Babies are not always the cuddly, cute figures seen in advertisements. They are selfish and demanding. Their crying can be constant and unexplainable. Teenage mothers who grow weary of this crying may physically or emotionally abuse their children.

Babies do not stay little for long. As they grow, their demands become more vocal. Food, medicine, diapers, day care, and clothing are just a few of the costs that make babies so expensive. Teenage mothers are usually unprepared for the amount of time needed to take care of a baby, and later a toddler.

Most teenage fathers do not get involved with taking care of the baby. The problem of raising a baby remains with the mother.

Many sexually active couples forget about the reality of a baby. Having and raising a baby is a life-changing, time-consuming process. It cannot be ignored.

Read the following letter. Based on what you have read, how would you respond to Ginny?

Dear Friend:

Remember that great-looking guy I met at the beach last summer? Well, we've been going out since last October. Chuck is fabulous—really the greatest. I'm in love! I know this is the real thing; it just has to be. How many fourteen-year-olds do you know who don't have a steady boyfriend?

Anyway, Chuck is just the greatest. My mom even likes him. Lately we've been getting a little more close—you know. I think it's really going to happen with him! I'm sort of scared, but excited at the same time. After all, sex is supposed to be a natural part of growing up. And, gosh, I've been growing up for years.

Well, I just had to let you know I'm alive and well.

Your friend, Ginny

Dear Ginny:

Happily Ever After

Sexual encounters portrayed in storybook romances on the media have a *happily ever after* ending. Sex supporters neglect to tell you the other side. Reality is not so happy.

These real-life people, with changed names, shared their stories. In each case, look at the long-term effects of sex prior to marriage.

• "I thought it would make him happy," Dotty confessed. She was four months pregnant when she and the baby's father married. They had been sexually active for almost a year. "What a mistake! All he does is scream at me about the baby and the house. Nothing I do makes him happy. He hates me; he hates our baby."

Soon after this conversation, Dotty discovered she was pregnant again. Her life grew even more miserable. The marriage was headed for divorce, when Dotty died suddenly of an unusual illness. She left her husband with three small children.

Dotty thought sex before marriage would help her keep her boyfriend. The problem was he was not worth keeping.

- "On our wedding night I kept thinking about how special this night was supposed to be." Jeff paused a long time, "But it wasn't anything special. Once we got engaged it seemed OK to have sex. Now I realized that magical night will never happen. It made me really sad."

Jeff was not the only one who felt deprived. Months later, Marcie shared her disappointment, "We tried to make it something different—you know a beautiful nightgown, music, the whole bit. But there was nothing new about it."

Jeff and Marcie missed the joy of waiting to share that unique first time together within the commitment of marriage.

- "Robert doesn't do it as expertly as my high school boyfriend did. Should I tell him what to do?" Her question surprised me. I thought Janice and Robert had the perfect marriage.

"When I was a high school sophomore, I dated a senior. We began having sex. He was great. Late in his senior year he was killed in an automobile accident. When I married Robert, I thought sex would be the same way. But he is so clumsy."

No one is born knowing how to do everything in life. In marriage both partners learn together about sexual techniques and how to please a mate. Actually the first sexual encounter between two inexperienced people can lack a lot of skill. *(Number 9 is false.)* Yet each knows there will be many years to become sex experts together.

Robert suffered unfairly from Janice's comparison. Janice decided to get a book that would help both of them learn how to express their needs.

- "I can't trust her. Every time she looks at another boy I get jealous." Kent had a right to be concerned. Prior to marriage both he and Cami had been sexually active. "How can I be sure she won't mess around while

I'm out of town or after we have a fight?"

Kent had a point. Sex experts agree that people who are sexually active prior to marriage are more likely to commit adultery within marriage. *(Number 10 is false.)* Kent never fully trusted Cami.

Teenagers live for the present. The future seems so far away. Yet, your decisions today influence your future. You must consider how present sexual actions might harm a marriage later.

Responsible Sex Results in Respectable Sexuality

When you are responsible about your sexuality, you respect yourself and others. Those who urge you to be sexually free refuse to face responsibility. They recommend sex whenever and with whomever you choose, regardless of what happens. You have seen, however, the variety of consequences of premarital sex.

You are responsible for keeping your body physically healthy and clean. You are responsible for maintaining your emotional health. You are responsible for your actions and how they affect others. The decisions you make now will help you in future commitments.

How can you know what is best for you? Well, first analyze the values taught to you by your family. These usually provide a good foundation for your own moral decisions.

• Identify your parents' moral values. What percentage of their money do you think your parents spend on the following?

____% possessions (cars, computers, etc.)
____% the church
____% education

____% charitable organizations (P.T.A., the Red Cross, March of Dimes, etc.)
____% entertainment

With *1* as most important and *14* as least important, rank the following items according to how you feel your parents value them.

_____ education
_____ sports achievement
_____ family
_____ church participation
_____ traditions
_____ job security
_____ money
_____ financial success
_____ business
_____ time with family
_____ television
_____ personal success
_____ friends
_____ personal pleasure

This shows you where you think your parents place their emphasis. Where they spend their money and what they hold as important indicate what they value.

Teenagers go through a process of beginning to form their own values. The values of parents exert a tremendous influence on the values of their children. Perhaps you do not totally agree with all your family's values. That's normal. In deciding on their own values, teenagers evaluate and sometimes question some of their parents' values. You are in the process of becoming. You are learning to be responsible for yourself. You cannot control your parents or their values. You can, however, hold on to the best values for yourself. During these teen years, your values may change. You will adopt values from people you admire. You may strengthen some values and do away with others. You can begin now to figure out what values seem best for you. If you are a Christian, you will want your personal values to be consistent with the teachings of the Bible.

- Decide what is important to you. List the top three things you treasure. These can be people, possessions, activities, or ideas.

1.

2.

3.

- Build friendships with people who encourage you to do your best. Work on developing a healthy self-worth. Feel good about who you are as a creation of worth in God's eyes. True friends help you maintain a positive image. They do not tear you down or try to convert you to their way of thinking.
- Avoid situations that can be trouble. Here is a good place to use the three tests of secrecy, universality, and prayer described in "Just Say No and Mean It" in the early part of this chapter.
- If you decide to adopt a new value, look at the consequences. As you make decisions on your own, you are expected to live with the consequences of your decisions. Some consequences are neither fun nor easy. You still have to accept them.
- Remember, you are in charge! God gave you a body, a mind, and a soul. With His help you can use these in the best possible way.

Answers to "In Love vs Sex Without Love" (pages 53-55)
In Love—3, 5, 7, 9, 13, 15
Sex Without Love—1, 2, 4, 6, 8, 10, 11, 12, 14

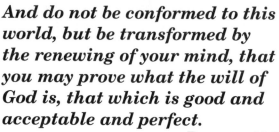

CHAPTER 4

Owner's Manual

And do not be conformed to this world, but be transformed by the renewing of your mind, that you may prove what the will of God is, that which is good and acceptable and perfect.

Romans 12:2

You bring it home encased in cardboard and plastic. It's just what you wanted. You have waited a long time. Today it is finally here.

Your fingers dig into the wrapping—popping tape, tugging away plastic covers. The first thing you see is the owner's manual. It warns, "To operate correctly, read the instructions."

Your sexuality is like that long-awaited package. It comes wrapped in a rapidly-changing body. You already have been reading about how to use this new, exciting part of you correctly. This is the final chapter of that manual.

Look for the answers to these true-false statements as you read this chapter.

   ____ 1. Teenagers want someone to love them.

   ____ 2. Having sex with someone results in a meaningful relationship.

_____ 3. Intimacy involves much more than sexual intimacy.

_____ 4. Liking to be with people of the same sex does not mean a person is homosexual.

_____ 5. Sexual abuse always involves intercourse.

_____ 6. In a typical teenage rape, both people know one another.

_____ 7. Prostitutes were associated with religion in ancient times.

_____ 8. Pornography is a harmless form of sexual expression.

_____ 9. True Christians do not ever desire sexual intercourse outside of marriage.

_____ 10. Sexual intercourse outside of marriage affects only two people.

Congratulations, Owner!

"Like a lily among the thorns,
So is my darling among the maidens.
Like an apple tree among the trees of the forest,
So is my beloved among the young men.
In his shade I took great delight and sat down.
And his fruit was sweet to my taste."

Do the preceding lines sound like a love poem? Well, it is a love poem. These lines from Song of Solomon 2:2-3 beautifully express a bride and groom's love for each other. This unique book in the Bible describes love in unusual images that sometimes sound strange.

These descriptions of love and sexuality in Song of Solomon affirm how God made sex good. God created sexuality and invented sexual expression. He understands the strong desire to bond with another person. He understands intimacy.

Intimacy, like love, is often misunderstood. It is tied up with people, their needs, and the desire for closeness.

People need these basics in life—air, food, water, cloth-

79

ing, and shelter. Beyond the basics, needs vary. People need exercise, but some require more than others. The same is true of acceptance of self, friendship, companionship, mental stimulation, and a closeness to God.

What about you? Rank the following needs on a scale of *1* to *6,* with *1* being your greatest need and *6* being your least need.

_____ acceptance of self

_____ a closeness to God

_____ friendship

_____ a happy home life

_____ someone to love me

_____ someone for me to love

Was that harder than you thought it would be? When asked to name their greatest need, one teenage group selected *someone to love me.* The desire for emotional closeness with another person is normal. It is called intimacy. *(Number 1 is true.)*

Intimacy lets you open yourself up without the fear of being hurt. You remove your mask. Emotionally, that intimate friend sees your fears and dreams and offers support. Spiritually, you share your doubts and hopes and find compassion. Mentally, you express theories and ideas and discover acceptance. The sexual union of marriage provides a level of physical intimacy that accompanies emotional, spiritual, and mental intimacy. In this sense, sexual intimacy expresses an intimate relationship and results in deeper intimacy and bonding. Physical intimacy alone, however, does not automatically result in the deepest levels of intimacy.

Teenagers want a close, caring association with someone of the opposite sex. That is natural. Unfortunately, some teenagers equate closeness with sex. They find it easier to jump into bed than to get to know another person. For these teenagers, it is easier to share a body than to share ideas, goals, common dreams. Many young people discover that after they have shared their bodies, they still long for the closeness and openness of intimacy.

(Number 3 is true.)

The world wants you to believe that having sex with someone results in a meaningful relationship with that person. In reality, two people can have sex and never have a relationship. *(Number 2 is false.)* They mate like animals in heat. They have no concern for one another.

On the other hand, two people can have a supportive, sharing relationship without sex. This friendship survives in good and bad times. Each desires the best for the other person. In fact, this warm friendship is essential for developing a healthy foundation for an excellent marriage.

So, congratulations! You now have the equipment to discover intimacy. Now proceed with caution.

Operate with Caution

Hopefully you have made the decision to remain pure until marriage. Terrific! That's a big step.

God created you and your hormones. Sexual desire is His idea. But God does not expect people to act like rabbits.

God gave you choice and the ability to know right and wrong. You decide how to fill your need for personal intimacy and how to handle sexual desire. One choice is to control that sexual desire until marriage. How difficult can that be?

If you were Ted or Lanie, would you:

Case Study: Lanie and Ted had several classes together and often shared notes. They hung out with the same kids at school. In the eighth grade Ted invited Lanie to his church. Soon she was active in many youth events. Gradually they spent time with just each other. One spring evening Lanie and Ted played on the swings at a nearby park. Their teasing ended up with them tussling on the ground. Suddenly Ted and Lanie moved to a deeper level of kissing than ever before. Each grappled frantically for the other's body. Time stopped.

1. Let things continue, thinking you can stop at any point? *(See Continuation A)*
2. Jump up, make a joke, and try to forget anything happened? *(See Continuation B)*
3. Be upset with yourself for having these strong sexual urges? *(See Continuation C)*

Continuation A—Things moved quickly. Before either realized it, they had sex. Later, when they said good night, each felt (circle your answer):
1. thrilled with their new relationship.
2. guilty and ashamed.
3. sad that they had gone this far.
What would you do now?

Continuation B—Both are embarrassed by their actions. They don't talk about it. The next time they are alone (circle your answer):
1. each thinks the other wanted the sexual involvement when in reality, neither did.
2. they move quickly to that same level of necking and petting.
3. they decide to break up.
What would you do now?

Continuation C—Both are overwhelmed by how close they came to making a mistake. They feel guilty for going so far. They fear that it might happen again. Together they ask their minister of youth for help. He reminds them that sexual feelings are normal. He suggests that they (circle your answer):
1. stay in public places, spending more time with others, than alone.
2. break up and date others.

82

3. forgive themselves and renew their commitments to remain pure.

What would you do now?

There is no final ending to this case study. Dealing with sexual feelings is a daily process. Your commitment to sexual purity will be tested frequently during your teen years. Because you are human, it's normal to sometimes be tempted to have sex before marriage. *(Number 9 is false.)* Because you are human, you can choose to wait and respond to that desire after you are married.

Sometimes people try to excuse their sexual behavior by saying they are "making love." Sexual intercourse is a physical act; it does not always involve love. Showing love, on the other hand, does not have to include sexual intercourse. There are many ways to demonstrate love. Which of the following have you used? What others can you think of?

____ cook the person's favorite food
____ give a small, simple gift like a single flower
____ participate in or watch the person's favorite sport
____ work on a project together
____ share a story
____ smile at the person across a room
____ frequently say that you care about the person
____ pray together
____ ask for help with a problem
____ compliment the person regularly
____ learn a new skill together

The statement *I love you* can also test your commitment. This simple sentence can be deceptive. Some repeat it casually. For others it has deep meaning. Many use it to manipulate and control. How does the emphasis on different words change the meaning of the sentence? Write its new meaning beside each sentence.

I love you.

I *love* you.

I love *you*.

Incorrect Product Information

Teenagers get about one-third of their sex education from peers. A second source of information is the movies. Often this is misinformation. Check out these myths.

• *Guys can't live without sex.* Some people live a life time without sex, even men. Many people direct their sexual energy into sports, business, academic excellence, or serving others.

• *It was love at first sight.* This kind of love makes up an imaginary relationship based on a person's physical appearance. Real love grows from friendship and knowledge, not a fantasy. I dated a boy for several months who finally stated, "It was love at first sight." He described the moment, "I saw you standing in the library, wrapped in that red coat, your hair messed up by the wind." I

The Right Word

Condom—A rubber covering that fits over the penis to keep sperm from fertilizing an egg.

Heterosexual—A person who is physically and sexually attracted to someone of the opposite sex.

Homosexual—A person who is physically and sexually attracted to someone of the same sex.

Sodomy—A legal term that refers to deviate sexual behavior other than normal intercourse.

stopped dating him soon after that. I've never owned a red coat.

• *Everybody's doing it!* Everyone is not doing it. The Center for Disease Control surveyed teenagers who were fifteen years old and younger. Only 27 percent of the girls and 33 percent of the boys said they have had premarital sex. That means two-thirds of the teenagers fifteen years old or younger are sexually pure.

If you hang around people who are sexually active, however, the peer pressure increases.

• *Having sex is an automatic part of growing up.* Sexual development is a large part of growing up. Sexual intercourse does not make you an adult. Mature adults control their bodies.

• *Guys need sexual experience.* The double standard that girls should be virgins and boys should be experienced still lives today. Both sexes can be informed without needing experience. It is exciting to learn the intricacies of sexual love with your marriage partner.

• *I owe him something for the date.* You have shared your time and friendship with him. Sex is never necessary to pay for a date.

• *Sex enhances a relationship.* Sex outside marriage actually damages a relationship. Guilt, fear of pregnancy, and deception compound the awkwardness and the unknown. The joy of sex best grows within a situation that is open and honest.

• *If I don't have sex, everyone will think I'm gay.* Sexual intercourse does not prove your femininity or masculinity. Your personality, actions, attitudes, and relationships confirm your sexuality. You don't need to prove a thing.

• *Safe sex is OK.* Makers of condoms would like you to believe this one. Surveys show, however, that condoms are only 88 to 98 percent effective. That remaining 2 to 12 percent of the time sperm and bodily fluids pass through. That increases the risk of pregnancy and sexually transmitted disease. When both of you wait until

Sex in the Bible

The Bible has a lot to say about sex. After God made man and woman, He blessed their physical union (Gen. 1:28). Men and women, however, managed to mess up a union God had blessed. The Bible records examples of sexual abuse and misuse. Each story points out how far the people drifted from God. One example is the corrupt story of Sodom in Genesis 19:1-15.

The Bible also records examples of sexual temptation. Some biblical heroes resisted temptation. Joseph hastily left when his boss's wife made a pass at him (Gen. 39:1-13). Other followers of God gave in to sexual temptation. Remember the sad story of David and Bathsheba in 2 Samuel 11:1-27? David not only committed adultery, but also murder and deception.

The New Testament also relates times when Jesus talked with those who had misused sex. In His meeting with the Samaritan woman at the well, He pointed out how she had abused her marriage vows (John 4:3-19).

Not all stories dealing with sex are bad. There are beautiful stories of love and marriage that affirm the goodness of sexuality. The Book of Ruth tells a haunting love story of sadness, faith, and caring. The Book of Hosea is an unusual story of love. Hosea loved his wife although she was unfaithful to him. Hosea compared the nation of Israel to his wife, and God's love to his love.

Some teenagers complain that the Bible does not deal with the realities of sex today. The Bible may not answer everyone's questions about sex and sexuality, but Bible truths don't change.

The following Scriptures state truths that relate to sex and sexuality. Match each of the statements with one of these Bible verses: (a) Galatians 5:19-21; (b) Romans 7:18-25; (c) 1 Corinthians 10:13; (d) Proverbs 18:22; (e) Psalm 24:4-5; (f) 1 Corinthians 7:2-4; (g) 1 Corinthians 6:18-20. Check your answers with those at the end of this chapter.

_____ 1. A husband and wife are responsible for meeting one another's sexual needs.

_____ 2. Christians constantly struggle with wanting to do right and actually doing wrong.

_____ 3. God will not let you be tempted beyond what you are able to handle.

_____ 4. A heart that is right with God provides the best foundation for right actions.

_____ 5. It's worth waiting for the right person who will be your husband or wife.

_____ 6. Resist sexual immorality because you and your body belong to God.

_____ 7. Sexual sins prove when a Christian's life is controlled by the world.

marriage, all sex is safe.

- *What the two of us do affects only us.* Remember the three tests of secrecy, universality, and prayer from Chapter 3? If sex is between just two people, then why do 250 million people contract sexually transmitted diseases each year? If sex is between just two people, then why do taxpayers support teenage mothers and their babies on welfare? If sex is between just two people, then why is tax-payers' money going for AIDS research? If sex is between just two people, then why is an abortion performed approximately every twenty seconds in the United States?

What a married couple does behind closed doors is between them. Sex outside of marriage has far-reaching influence. *(Number 10 is false.)*

Product Misuse

Incorrect information about sex confuses young people. Sexual misuse adds to that confusion. You already have seen how premarital sex misuses God's intended purpose for sex. Other misuses go against God's plan for healthy sexuality.

Sexual Abuse

Sexual abuse is any sexual activity against a person without that person's consent. Consent requires two parts: (1) understanding what a person agrees to do; and (2) the freedom to say yes or no. Abuse takes away that freedom.

Sexual abuse may or may not involve intercourse. Inappropriate touching and fondling are also considered sexual abuse. *(Number 5 is false.)* Physical and emotional abuse may accompany sexual abuse. Physical abuse includes slapping, pushing, or any aggressive physical behavior. Emotional abuse includes name calling, screaming, and attempts to control the one being abused.

Professionals believe that one in four girls and one in eight boys have been sexually abused during childhood or early adolescence. Almost 90 percent of all sexual abuse is committed by someone known by the family. These could be neighbors, family friends, or relatives not living in the home. Two-thirds of those were abused by someone living in the home. Sexual abuse by a relative is incest.

Most sexual abuse occurs prior to the teen years. During the crucial youth years of development, however, prior abuse has damaging effects. It can tear down a teen's self-esteem. Abused teenagers may deny or minimize the abuse. Sometimes they think they deserved it. Many times they want to protect the abusing family member.

Younger teenagers are susceptible to abuse. Because they hunger for affection, they sometimes accept sexual abuse as one way of finding love.

It takes great courage to tell a trusted adult information about sexual abuse. Talk with a parent, a trusted Christian adult, a minister, or a teacher. Young people who have experienced this cruel behavior need professional help from a Christian counselor.

Case Study: When Sandy moved to your town, you became instant friends. You spend your free time together. Sandy comes over to your house frequently, but never invites you to hers. One night while watching a story about sexual abuse on TV, Sandy tells you that she has been sexually abused. How would you feel about Sandy's situation? What would you say to Sandy?

Sexual Assault and Rape

The broadest definition of sexual assault covers all sexual behavior forced on a person. This includes rape, incest, sodomy, oral sex, and fondling.

Rape is a crime of violence. A person is forced to have sexual intercourse. Women are the primary target, although men can also be raped by a man. Most rapists are not seeking sexual pleasure. They only want to control and humiliate the other person.

Approximately one million females are raped each year. Law enforcement officials guess at this number, because 80 percent of the rape victims don't report this crime. Many teenage boys are also raped each year by older men. This crime also goes unreported.

A typical teenage rape involves a boyfriend (date rape) or an acquaintance. *(Number 6 is true.)* These rapes most often occur in the victim's home, the offender's home, or a car. Drinking and drugs are often involved.

Statutory rape is a legal situation. This is sexual intercourse where the victim is under the age of consent and the suspect is at least four calendar years older than the

Why Stay Pure?

You have good, solid reasons for saying *no* to peer pressure. You have discovered moral and religious reasons, as well as physical ones. The following nine reasons have been stressed in this book. Unscramble the scrambled words to remind yourself why it is important to remain pure. Check out the answers at the end of this chapter.

1. to *yeob Gsdo rdWo*
2. for your *utruef geararim*
3. because of *fels peersct*
4. to keep a *mintomcemt* to *truipy*
5. to avoid *xleysaul stidatntmer adessie*
6. to avoid *grecynnap*
7. to avoid a decision about *taniboor*
8. to avoid *litug*
9. to avoid *cloopgschialy* and *laintoome agedma*

victim. In most states, the legal age of consent is eighteen. Aggravated rape is where the victim is under thirteen.

Rape counselors encourage girls to be careful. Girls should be sure that neither their actions nor their appearances give off false sexual messages.

Remember, you are responsible for your body. You have the right to say no to any kind of sexual pressure.

Case Study: Your brother comes home from college and brings a friend from his fraternity. One evening the guys brag about their dates. The friend tells how he got a girl drunk and had sex with her. They laugh at how upset she was when she realized what had happened. How would you feel listening to this conversation? What could you say to your brother and his friend?

Pornography

Pornography is a difficult area to define. Changing federal and state laws confuse the issue. The broadest definition of pornography includes any sexually explicit material designed for sexual arousal. This can be movies (including R-rated movies), literature, magazines, art, and music.

Pornography is harmful because it often degrades women, glamorizes male dominance, and depicts the practice of violence against women. *(Number 8 is false.)* Pornography is mainly produced for the heterosexual male.

Different words are associated with pornography, although they may not fit the legal definition. Soft-core pornography is socially acceptable to some people. Hard-core pornography takes a "no-holds-barred" approach to all kinds of deviate and abusive sex portrayals. Obscenity, erotica, and X-rated are other terms that are used. Dial-a-porn makes verbal pornography available to anyone who can dial a telephone, including children.

Case Study: John is spending the night with Steven. When Steven takes John to his parents' bedroom, closes the door, and pulls out some magazines from under the bed, John recognizes the names as being popular pornography magazines. Steven starts showing John the pictures. If you were John, how would you feel in this situation? What would you say or do?

Prostitution

Prostitution has been called the world's oldest profession. Prostitution is sexual activity exchanged for something else, usually money, but often drugs or food. This sexual activity is promiscuous, casual, and indifferent.

In ancient cultures prostitutes often were linked to religion. Since many religions revolved around the harvest season, they thought prostitutes ensured fertility. *(Number 7 is true.)*

Females become prostitutes for many reasons. Mainly they lack the skills needed to earn a living. Some sell their bodies to support drug and alcohol addictions. Others have run away from home. A few are forced to work for a boyfriend.

There are also male prostitutes. They sell their bodies to women or to homosexual men.

Homosexuality

Homosexuals prefer sexual activity with partners of the same sex. Men who prefer men are called gays. Women who prefer women are called lesbians.

Homosexuality is not new. It was commonly practiced in the pagan world, and especially in Rome. Early caesars practiced homosexuality.

The Jewish religion held up God's will for male and female to mate. Laws emerged condemning sexual misuses, including homosexuality (Lev. 18—21).

In the New Testament Paul was most vocal about homosexuality. In Romans 1:26-32 and 1 Corinthians

6:9, he condemned this activity as violating God's plan for man and woman to complete one another sexually.

In this critical time of sexual development in teenagers, some are confused about their sexual feelings. It is not unusual for teenagers your age to prefer friends of the same sex. That does not mean those teenagers are homosexual. *(Number 4 is true.)*

Jesus held up the ideal home where a man and woman leave their parents and come together as husband and wife (Matt. 19:4-6). But Jesus also told Christians to love their neighbors (Luke 10:27). A person loves that neighbor, but not the neighbor's deeds. Christians can show compassion and concern for those whose life-style is different, without accepting their sexual acts.

Case Study: The guys always tease Charlie because he's so small. You and Charlie were best friends in grades four and five, but in the last few years you've found different interests. Lately the guys have been calling Charlie a *homo* because he won't ask a girl for a date. You know they're just teasing. How would you feel about the situation? What would you do or say to Charlie or to the other guys?

Lifetime Warranty

A warranty promises that the product is guaranteed to work for a specific time, such as ninety days, one year, or 50,000 miles. It assures the purchaser that the products will work. God's warranty guarantees forgiveness that is good for a lifetime. Maybe you have committed a sexual sin. God offers forgiveness. To receive that forgiveness you must truly want to change. Then you must confess your sin.

God's forgiveness is noted throughout the Bible. After

Quick Advice for Staying Pure

When my parents say no, that's when I say yes. Is that how you react to your parents' advice? If you won't listen to parents, consider these words from teenagers like you. They share advice about times when they became involved in sexual situations.

• Be careful. Clothing gets you in trouble. Some clothing sends powerful sexual messages that say *I'm ready!*— especially in warm weather, when you wear less clothing and skimpy bathing suits. Do you wear a sexual invitation?

• Stay with a group. Don't leave with someone you hardly know.

• Watch those roaming hands. State your sexual limits before any inappropriate sexual activity begins.

• Remember that lots of heavy kissing, especially when you're tired, leads to trouble every time.

• Plan your dates. Suggest places to go and things to do. Empty time is boring. Boredom leaves time for the wrong things to happen.

• Stay away from drugs, alcohol, and make-out parties. They take away your ability to think clearly. You'll be caught in a sexual situation and won't know how to get out.

• Leave if you don't like the way a date is going. Call a friend or a parent if you need a ride home. Avoid being a sexual statistic.

David's sexual sin with Bathsheba, he wrote about God's forgiveness in Psalm 51—in verses 3-4 he confessed his sin and in verses 10-13 he asked for God's forgiveness. In John 8:3-11, John recorded the story of how Jesus forgave sexual sin.

Whatever sin you have committed, God can forgive you. Fill in the following prayer as a guideline for asking for that forgiveness.

Holy Lord,
I come before you today aware of my sin. (Read 1 John 1:9.) I confess the sin of

Read 2 Corinthians 5:17. Write a sentence stating how you want to be new.

Read Philippians 4:13. Write a sentence about how God can help you.

Read 1 Corinthians 6:18 and 1 John 2:3,15. Write a sentence stating what you can do to prevent the sin for happening again.

Read Hebrews 10:23. Thank God for His promise.

Amen.

All You Ever Wanted to Know About Sex, But Were Afraid to Ask

You are almost to the end of this book. Hopefully, this book has answered many of your questions, relieved or lessened your fears, and aided you in learning something to help you become the sexual being God wants you to be.

Summarize what you have studied by completing these sentences.

One thing I learned is . . .

I learned that my body . . .

I learned that the opposite sex . . .

The information that surprised me was . . .

The information that helped me was . . .

Have you made a commitment to yourself and to God to remain sexually pure until marriage? If so, take the time to fill out this card. Ask a friend to sign it as a witness to your commitment.

I, _____, on this date _____ have decided to remain sexually pure until I marry. I will try to avoid sexually tempting situations. I will not give in to peer pressure. I will seek to be the best person I can by obeying God's call for purity.

Signed: _____

In the presence of: _____

Answers to "Sex in the Bible" (pages 86-87)
1. f; 2. b; 3. c; 4. e; 5. d; 6. g; 7. a.

Answers to "Why Stay Pure?" (page 90)
1. obey God's word; 2. future marriage; 3. self-respect; 4. commitment to purity; 5. sexually transmitted disease; 6. pregnancy; 7. abortion; 8. guilt; 9. psychological, emotional damage.